D0913307

AFRICAN WISDOM

101 Proverbs from the Motherland

✳

Tokunbo Adelekan

Judson Press
Valley Forge

African Wisdom: 101 Proverbs from the Motherland

Judson Press has made every effort to trace the ownership of all quotes. In the event of
a question arising from the use of a quote, we regret any error made and will be pleased to
make the necessary correction in future printings and editions of this book.

Bible quotations in this volume are from *The Holy Bible*, King James Version. (KJV); the
New American Bible, copyright © 1970, 1986, 1991 by the Confraternity of Christian Doc-
trine, 3211 Fourth Street, N.E., Washington, D.C. 20017. All rights reserved. (NAB); the
New American Standard Bible, © 1960, 1962, 1963, 1968, 1971, 1972, 1973, 1975, 1977
by The Lockman Foundation. Used by permission. (NASB); HOLY BIBLE: *New International Version*, copyright © 1973, 1978, 1984. Used by permission of Zondervan Bible Pub-
lishers. (NIV); The New King James Version. Copyright © 1972, 1984 by Thomas Nelson
Inc. (NKJV); the New Revised Standard Version of the Bible, copyright © 1989 by the Division of Christian Education of the National Council of the Churches of Christ in the United States of America. Used by permission. All rights reserved. (NRSV); and the Revised
Standard Version of the Bible, copyright © 1946, 1952, 1971, by the Division of Christian
Education of the National Council of the Churches of Christ in the U.S.A. Used by permission. (RSV)

Library of Congress Cataloging-in-Publication Data

Adelekan, Tokunbo.
   African wisdom : 101 proverbs from the motherland / Tokunbo Adelekan.— 1st ed.
   p. cm.
   ISBN 0-8170-1461-6 (alk. paper)
   1. Christian life—Meditations. 2. Proverbs, African. I. Title.
   BV4501.3.A34 2004
   398.9'096—dc22

                                                                        2004001680

10 09 08 07 06 05 04
10 9 8 7 6 5 4 3 2 1

To Adetunji Adelekan and Patricia Adelekan,
loving parents and learned citizens whose wisdom and
work continues to inspire generations to
experience the luminous depths of Africa.

And to Tahira Olu Funke Nadine Adelekan,
whose life continues to hum the melody of sacrifice.

Contents

Acknowledgments

This text is the product of many heads, hands, and hearts. Without the editorial guidance of Randy Frame this book would never have materialized. I'm truly indebted to him. I also want to thank Charlemagne Nditemeh, my soul brother and alter-ego, whose sober research and searching comments have added to the quality of the text. Much appreciation also goes to Diane Vescovi, whose diligence and organization streamlined the work and contributed to its style.

I am grateful to Jeron Frame and Elaine Anne MacGgregor for their thorough readings of the early text. I am especially thankful to Drew Ludwig, whose journalistic talents helped make the work friendly to a broad readership. Also I thank Sheri Magness, Tracy Duncan, Mipo Dadang, and Rosamund Atta-Fynn, wonderful students who have allowed me to grow alongside them in ministry and learning. I want to express my gratitude to Muyiwa Omololu and Tayo Ogun, both of whom pressed me to deepen my understanding of West African cultural philosophy in general and Yoruba moral perspectives in particular.

I acknowledge Ryszard Pachocinski, whose book *Proverbs of Africa: Human Nature in the Nigerian Oral Tradition* was the source for several of the proverbs I chose. I thank Clarence James, Johnny Ray Youngblood, Ed Taylor, J. Wendell Mapson, and Larry Markus—all luminaries in the contemporary black church—for their helpful comments throughout the project.

Finally, I want to thank my loving wife, Tahira, for her poignant and profound comments from the beginning to the end.

Foreword

The spirit of a people gives birth to its wisdom. This spirit emerges from the depths of their experience, then takes form in various modes of communication. The proverb is one of the most enduring forms and universal expressions of the collective wisdom of humanity. It is the most flexible and accessible as well. Like a snapshot, each proverb captures a depth of insight that illuminates a variety of life situations from a variety of different angles.

Through a series of these snapshots taken of the African spirit, Dr. Adelekan has fashioned a collage that allows us to glimpse the depths of African wisdom. In this collage, African Americans will hear the echoes of our Mothers', Fathers', and extended families' voices as they have shaped and equipped us to deal with the harsh realities of life in oppression. Others will likewise hear the profoundly human voice calling out of the continent that gave birth to life as we know it; a continent that has known more than its share of the suffering of humanity and yet has responded with a wisdom that breeds endurance and a joy borne of a beauty baptized in pain.

Dr. Adelekan has performed an invaluable service. He has provided us with a profound resource for meditation and practice that will enrich immeasurably our spiritual praxis. The careful selection of the proverbs he shares reflects the wisdom of the spirit that developed them.

Matthew V. Johnson Sr.
Adjunct Assistant Professor in Religious Studies, Wake Forest University
and Pastor of Manasseh Baptist Church, Greensboro, North Carolina

Introduction

The cloth of life is interwoven with the threads of language. To be human is to speak. To traffic in the currency of language is therefore to engage in risky business. And for those of us who are called to live "recklessly" for God, speech, while a risk of faith, is also a gift of sheer grace. Speech opens up the human spirit to new vistas of growth, harmony, and transcendence.

The use of proverbs in human speech bears witness to human risk taking. Proverbs both clarify and confound, ushering us into new pastures of human experience and enlightenment. Herein lies the majestic and mysterious power of the proverb.

The ancient Hebrews, who were renowned for their learning, had the unique genius of packaging pithy and profound statements into nutshells of images. Proverbs embody and exemplify, celebrate and convey wisdom in a way that is accessible to all. The beauty and imagery of a proverb is its main attraction, yet it supplies much more. Proverbs are wisdom incarnate. They are repositories for moral vision, spiritual potency, and existential pabulum, and as such they are necessary for responsible human living.

African proverbs, like Hebrew maxims, are works of moral art and linguistic dexterity. They give meaning to the human situation in a manner inaccessible through most other modes of communication. African proverbs, in particular, are celebrated for their sense of depth and foresight, their homespun sagacity, their moral character, their respect for elders and family, and above all their worship of God. They are characterized by a holistic approach to life and learning, serving as a coping mechanism for those left at the perils of jealousy, tribulation, tragedy, death, dread, and despair—in short, the whole range of human experience.

Among the Yoruba it is said that "a proverb is the horse of conversation; when the conversation lags, a proverb revives it." It is a horse that transports us to fresh plateaus of expansion, creativity, and mutuality. Among the Ibo, a proverb is seen as cultural seasoning. It invites those who partake of it to savor otherwise hidden aspects of the feast of life. If language is the stuff of life, proverbs invigorate life with meaning. As speech is the stuff of life, so wisdom is the stuff of proverbs. We do well to heed the instruction of King Solomon,

> The beginning of wisdom is this: Get wisdom,
>> and whatever else you get, get insight. (Proverbs 4:7, NRSV)

Though the proverbs chosen for this volume vary in degree, texture, and tone, they share a common thread. All convey insight and instructions for dignified existence and serve as a moral compass for a pilgrim's progress.

There are those who place a wedge between African spirituality and the teachings of Scripture. In many parts of Europe and North America it is still widely believed that before the coming of the first missionaries, Africans were bound by such practices as fetishism, animism, or some vulgar form of polytheism. We do not share this view. Such perspectives on African faith practices fail to appreciate the complexity and profundity of traditional African belief systems within which God-talk was central.

For the overwhelming number of African peoples, God stands alone as the one supreme parent, creator, and sustainer of the universe. In fact it is believed that "no one has to teach a child that God exists" (see proverb 96). When a child witnesses the rising and setting of the sun, admires the undulating waves of the ocean, or catches the mighty eagle as it swims across the bosom of the eastern sky, he or she sees that there is a God.

Just as there are physical laws in the universe, so there are moral laws. God confers order, a purpose, that orchestrates its moral locomotion. This alone restores hope. It reminds us that "God does not leave God's child tied up overnight" (see proverb 89).

John Mbiti, Bolaji Idowu, Mercy Amba Oduyoye, and others have argued that in the African worldview there is no fundamental distinction between the secular and the sacred. These proverbs testify to this truth. They speak to the fact that the sacred pervades every aspect of life. There is no realm or sphere that is not understood without reference to God's sacred order.

Another widely held belief among African peoples is that human beings come into the world with the potential for both good and evil. A person becomes good through spiritual training and moral development. In short, goodness is virtue that must be worked on and worked for. To be a good person, one must develop the discipline to control unruly desires and the dedication to stand and ward off temptation.

The dangers of this world are many, but the good person typically follows the path of wisdom. This is also the path that leads to prosperity and peace. It is the most trusted of paths. It is the path of the elders. Yet those who refuse the path are neither forsaken nor forfeited; they are still held within the embrace of God's grace.

These proverbs are full of advice on how to build human relationships. The African moral imagination places a premium on interdependence, solidarity, and community. Human beings need one another and must depend on one another as a way of being witnesses to God's covenant with them. Life is interrelated. We are all part of the grand conversation of humanity. God is its author. As Dr. Martin Luther King Jr. was fond of saying, "We are caught up in an inescapable garment of mutuality woven by a single thread of destiny. What affects one directly affects all indirectly."

This book marks the beginning of an effort by a young African Christian intellectual, nurtured in the African American experience, to weave together three distinguishable yet inseparable moral traditions: African, African American, and biblical. My father is of Yoruba extraction, raised in an Anglican household. My mother, an African American from Columbus, Ohio, was born into a family thoroughly involved in the Catholic life of faith and remains true to her African culture. These two cultural streams (the African and the African American) are regulated and refined by my commitment to obey the love ethic of Jesus Christ and to fully live the requirements of the kingdom of God. As

Psalm 46 declares, "There is a river whose streams make glad the city of God" (verse 4, NRSV). In this sense this book is a way of keeping open the conversation between Africa and America on the grand subject of Christianity.

African Wisdom is hardly a book about African history, yet it serves the purpose of history. Its aim is to keep tradition alive through the living of a story in the making. By talking about life, it extends life. By commenting upon the present, it opens us to the future and it opens the future to us. This conversation is not mere human speech; it is speech about the ultimate meaning, the final purpose of life. It relives and extends the past by making a contribution to the rich litany of songs and utterances that texture meaning.

The proverbs included here represent the traditional folk wisdom and religions of sub-Saharan Africa. Since African proverbs are constantly being redefined, revisited, and recast to fit new social realities, it has proved difficult to preserve these truths in their classical form. Nevertheless, I have tried to render them in a manner that is both true to traditional wisdom and communicable to contemporary audiences. Many of the proverbs in this book are known to have originated with a particular ethnic group or area in Africa. In cases where I do not specify an area of origin, the proverb is commonly known in various parts of the African continent and the specific area of origin is not known.

In understanding the essence and purpose of African proverbs, the phrase "bright songs in dark nights" is especially meaningful to me. These words, uttered by no other than the biblical Job, express the African story in the Americas. It is the grammar of faith. The words flow from the wellsprings of great sorrow. They issue from the tongue of one who has been stripped of status and standing in life, one whose spiritual sores are fresh from the winds of change.

The book of Job expresses the cry of one who had come to life's edge to peer into the abyss while refusing to fall in. This tale signifies defiance and deliverance, heart and hope, fortitude and faithfulness. It reflects the uncanny ability to draw upon unseen powers in order to overcome painfully dismal odds. It indicates the refusal to surrender to a hopeless hope. It represents an attempt to wager one's sanity against the fangs of despair. It is indeed a hope against hope.

Many African American preachers have used Job as the symbol of the black experience in America—the episodic lapse from prosperity; the cataclysmic fall into chattel slavery; the chronic blues feeling that accompanies being viewed as a problem (W.E.B. DuBois). Yet the black experience in its response to these dismal happenings manifests an unflagging desire to acknowledge the God of history, the Creator God, who gives us songs in dark nights. How remarkable are these words that defy the authorship of human beings? Persistent self-expression through protracted misery constitutes an attempt to brace suffering with wisdom, to match poetry with pain, to etch out transcendence through the power of the spirit. A song in the dark night reveals the expressiveness of blacks who dared to sing the Lord's song in a strange language.

The complex experiences that frame the black story in the New World include colonialism, imperialism, the slave trade, and slavery itself. Yet the critical question is not what happened but how this great evil was overcome; not the mounting of despair but the testament of hope. How did Africans brought to the New World draw upon their African God-consciousness in ways that allowed them to come up with bright songs in dark nights?

This book suggests that one critical way was through the preservation of the wisdom tradition, that body of knowledge that through sanctified imagination allowed the human spirit to soar to the heights of transcendence, creativity, and fellowship with the divine. Hence, proverbs were bright songs. They constitute survival and transcendence, fortitude and faith, hope and heart. This brand of Christianity on the contemporary African scene speaks to the deep resonance that the African genius has for New Testament teachings.

May we all be blessed with such radiant streams. And as we travel through this barren land to a land filled with milk and honey, may we recognize that the timeless wisdom of African spirituality in its raw, robust purity is worthy of our reflection.

PART ONE

"Somebody Prayed for Me":

Human Character
and Conduct

The frog wanted to be as big as the elephant and burst.
(Nigeria)

✴

Imitation is not flattery but suicide. Greed is a drug. These two vices conspire wherever God's identity is ignored, and they breed death.

Greed multiplied by imitation leads down the path of death and destruction. It reflects a lack of self-worth, a problem with envy, and a lack of appreciation for one's God-given identity. The human attempt to over-step our boundaries reflects a spirit of pride and rebellion. To know one's place is humility. A true servant's trademark is submission to the workings of the Spirit.

* * *

Present yourselves to God.... Present your members to God as instruments of righteousness. (Romans 6:13, NRSV)

The miserly man is like a fattened ox—he will give of his fat
only when he has been deprived of his life.

✳

Our age is an age of never-ending consumption. We love to acquire. Our
desires drive us. Our eyes rule us. Our stomachs enslave us. Our love for
more is eclipsed only by our reluctance to share.

The main character in the movie *Scarface* (brilliantly played by Al Paci-
no) never had enough. No matter how much he acquired, he always wanted more. But when he finally shared of his largess, it was too late. After his
vast empire lay in ruins, his estranged wife left him, his sister and mother iso-
lated him, his friends betrayed him, and his body was riddled with bullets.

Death should never be the prerequisite for soulful surrender. Submission to
the Spirit should be the oxygen by which the Christian lives. We must remember that Christianity is a gift; our salvation is presented to us free of charge.
Hence, the index of a Christian's faithfulness consists of openness to the Spirit, a capacity to give, and gratitude. These qualities flow from the fruit of the
Spirit: love, patience, gentleness, kindness, and more (Galatians 5:22-23).

Walls that are built to exclude others, no matter how strong they are, will
eventually crumble. This is why greed and racism are pathogens that destroy
their carriers. We are called to be wise and watchful stewards. We should
deploy our resources so as to empower and enlighten others. There must
always be enough to go around. This is the foundation of Christ's ministry and
the bedrock of the kingdom.

✳   ✳   ✳

Now the whole group of those who believed were of one heart and soul, and no
one claimed private ownership of any possessions, but everything they owned
was held in common. (Acts 4:32, NRSV)

The prosperity of the trees is the well-being of the birds.

✳

In a sermon, John Claypool, a renowned Episcopalian preacher, announced that when he was young he thought that to be blessed meant to occupy privileged position, to sit in the lap of luxury, and to be pampered. He thought that his sister was blessed because she was spoiled by a particular relative. As an adult, though, he spoke to a firefighter who gave him a new understanding of the term *blessed*. The firefighter said that when one is asked by a superior officer to do a difficult job or to perform a demanding feat, that person is considered blessed.

There are two definitions of the word *blessed*. One is based on the self and on self-service—that is, on what one is getting. The other is based on others—on what one is giving. One is self-centered and the other is other-regarding.

Have any birds flown into your tree seeking food and shelter lately? Check your spirit of service.

* * *

"What is the kingdom of God like? And to what should I compare it? It is like a mustard seed that someone took and sowed in the garden; it grew and became a tree, and the birds of the air made nests in its branches." (Luke 13:18-19, NRSV)

4

Knowledge is not the main thing, but deeds are.

✳

"Do you know that saying is true?" asked Mr. Ozie of his son, whose head was bowed. James had just squandered his book allowance. He had indulged his passion for games. James nodded his head in agreement. He was ashamed, hurt. Once again his need to fit in, to impress his schoolmates, had gotten the better of him. He was afraid to look up and meet his father's gaze.

"Then why did you spend all of your money on video games, *knowing* that you were supposed to use some of it on books? You must take the games back to the store and *do* the right thing."

Do The Right Thing was the title of Spike Lee's film of ten years ago. It speaks to an enduring human problem: we know the truth, but we do not do it. We are hearers but not doers. Our problem is the ever-present thorn of disobedience, laziness, or smugness.

Dwight D. Eisenhower once quipped, "Don't let your learning lead to knowledge; let your learning lead to action." A person may know the truth, but unless that person speaks the truth, innocent people often become victims. It is insufficient for us to claim that we know Christ without fulfilling his works. We can no longer pose simply as hearers of the Word. True understanding, for the believer, is expressed in concerted and wise action. Head, heart, and hand combine to form the glorious trinity of Christian action.

* * *

Faith by itself, if it has no works, is dead. (James 2:17, NRSV)

* * *

Anyone . . . who knows the right thing to do and fails to do it, commits sin. (James 4:17, NRSV)

No matter how good, what you produce is better.
(Kagoma)

＊

Work dignifies. It blesses the hands, head, and heart that produce it. That is why the ancients said that labor provides healing to the soul. Work also increases self-confidence and a sense of self-worth.

Take ownership of what God has given you. Invest your labor with your spirit. Your work is a calling or vocation. It must consume you. In fact, at a certain point, you do not own your calling; rather, your calling owns you. It is something that calls you to a higher level of spirituality and discipleship.

If God has entrusted you with something, the elements of the universe move into neutral, waiting for you to deliver. This is why Jeremiah said, "Within me there is something like a burning fire shut up in my bones" (Jeremiah 20:9, NRSV). God expects you, by the power of divine grace, to improve upon your situation through work.

God desires this because God seeks to bless your life. Hence your responsibilities are not stumbling blocks; they are stepping-stones to fruitful living. This is the essence of stewardship.

＊   ＊   ＊

A slack hand causes poverty, but the hand of the diligent makes rich. (Proverbs 10:4, NRSV)

＊   ＊   ＊

Jesus looked at them and said, "For mortals it is impossible, but for God all things are possible." (Matthew 19:26, NRSV)

＊   ＊   ＊

We know that in all things God works for the good of those who love him, who have been called according to his purpose. (Romans 8:28, NIV)

A feeble effort will not fulfill the self.
(Dogon)

*

Shortcuts often short-circuit. When we sacrifice hard work, often the first casualty is dignity. Perhaps that is why Aesop declared, "Self-help is the best help." Misery is often the child of laziness, while hard work brings its own rewards. Not so with shiftlessness. Many people regret the wrong investment of their energies way after it is too late. However, this proverb extends far beyond hard work. Feebleness not only has to do with paucity of effort but also with the worth of its direction. Earnest effort has much to do with what we do when we have opportunity:

Do you have the resources to help the hungry? Feed God's children.

Do you have the opportunity to help the weak? Empower and help them.

Is it necessary to speak the truth even when it is unpopular? Speak it!

Can you help out a youngster? Spare the time.

Can you give hope to a discouraged heart? Speak a word of love.

God has given us an abundance of blessings. They take a number of guises: a hurt friend, a needy student, an estranged foreigner, a rejected child, an ignored elder, an unwritten poem, an unforgiven person, an unloved father, a dying ministry. We ignore or evade them at our own peril. We bless ourselves by blessing others. When we bless half-heartedly, the first casualty is the self.

Benjamin Elijah Mays said that we make our living by what we get; we make our lives by what we give.

*   *   *

"You did not choose me but I chose you. And I appointed you to go and bear fruit, fruit that will last, so that the Father will give you whatever you ask him in my name." (John 15:16, NRSV)

He who conceals his disease cannot expect to be cured.
(Ethiopia)

✳

We are all lepers. We carry our sores with us. Some of these sores are tattooed to the body; some are imprinted on the soul. Some of us are brave enough to expose them in order to heal them. Most of us would rather not. We mistake comfort for cure. The problem is that our cover becomes our killer.

Acknowledgment is the first step to healing. That is why physicians pronounce a diagnosis before they perform an operation. We must be bold enough to face the consequences. Remember, from a spiritual point of view, faith is the source of healing. That is why Jesus told the woman with the issue of blood, "Your faith has made you well" (Matthew 9:22, NRSV). She was brave enough to declare her ailment and to seek help. Many thousands have not had the faith to face their sin and try Jesus. When you turn to Jesus, you free your soul and body from unnecessary burdens that eventually can destroy you and your loved ones.

* * *

No one shall be able to stand against you all the days of your life. As I was with Moses, so I will be with you; I will not fail you or forsake you. (Joshua 1:5, NRSV)

* * *

Confess your sins to one another, and pray for one another, so that you may be healed. The prayer of the righteous is powerful and effective. (James 5:16, NRSV)

Men fall only to rise.
(West Africa)

✳

Failure is the great informant: it tells us where success is not. Hence it points us indirectly to the land of possibility.

Dr. William Augustus Jones, of the Bethany Baptist Church in New York, once said, "A setback is only a setup for a comeback." Failure can be used as a stepping-stone to faith. It is a lesson that breathes wisdom into the soul—a veritable mind sharpener.

Many great people have learned this lesson. Muhammad Ali lost his belt twice but came back to become the most celebrated heavyweight champion of all time. Clyde Drexler did not win an NBA championship until late in his career, after several failed attempts. Toni Morrison experienced several personal tragedies prior to her recognition as a Nobel laureate.

The Bible is a portfolio of people who, by the power of God, told despair and defeat to take a hike. Joseph's life is a profile of falling and rising. Moses failed miserably early in life; that is why he had to leave Egypt. Saul was passionately wrongheaded until he met Jesus. Jesus got up from the grave with all power in his hands.

* * *

Our steps are made firm by the LORD, when he delights in our way; though we stumble, we shall not fall headlong, for the LORD holds us by the hand. (Psalm 37:23-24, NRSV)

Do a thing at its time and peace follows it.
(Mandinka)

✳

Work provides healing to the soul. Jesus fed off it: "My food is to do the will of him who sent me [the Father]" (John 4:34, NRSV).

Those imbued with a sense of purpose do not shun planned activity, concerted action, or purposeful work. With a goal in mind, work provides joy, sustenance, meaning, and the means of living. Work is so important that the Scripture seems to abhor shiftlessness. There is an alarming clarity to the Savior's words: "Every branch in me that beareth not fruit he taketh away: and every branch that beareth fruit, he purgeth it, that it may bring forth more fruit" (John 15:2, KJV). In short, work is central to the building of the kingdom, which is our purpose for living.

Productive work builds character and gives one a sense of moral, social, and psychological worth.

* * *

I can do all things through Christ which strengtheneth me. (Philippians 4:13, KJV)

* * *

Perseverance must finish its work, so that you may be pure and complete, not lacking anything. (James 1:4, NIV)

Whatever accomplishment you boast of in the world, there is someone better than you.
(West Africa)

✳

Low is the way. As the cliché goes, "The folk you pass going up the ladder of life are the same folk you pass going back down the ladder of life." That is why it is more important to cultivate a mentality of appreciation than one of arrogance. When you develop a mindset that affirms accomplishments and achievements, you are in prime position to realize how good the Lord is.

Human beings were created in a garden for a reason. A garden is a place of multiplicity, variety, and dynamism. We all have different gifts. And so, no matter how gifted you are, there are others who are more gifted. This is not cause to despair; it is reason to celebrate. Be thankful for how the Lord is operating in the lives of others. If God did not operate in the lives of others, how would we survive?

People are our greatest blessing. God chose human flesh as a way to redeem the world. Look at music, sports, and medicine—thank God that blessings do not begin and end with you. This is a key ingredient of faithfulness. To know this is to accept and appreciate the limitations built into the fabric of human achievement. Jehovah alone is supreme.

*　　*　　*

By the grace given to me I say to everyone among you not to think of yourself more highly than you ought to think, but to think with sober judgment, each according to the measure of faith that God has assigned. (Romans 12:3, NRSV)

II

Message is not an eye.
(Igala)

✳

"Be yourself." Good advice. But it's much easier said than done. Which self? The one my parents dictated? The one defined by my race? By my gender?

It is important that you assert your own identity and individuality in thought and initiate your own projects in deeds.

The Igala say, "Message is not an eye." In other words, you may hear something, but no matter how credible it may seem, hearing about it is not the same as being an eyewitness to the event. Likewise, many things in life will be done for you. However, there is nothing like the work of one's own hands.

Trust your own judgment. As Dr. Matthew Johnson once told an eager student, "Follow another person's lead, but not to their house." Truth can only be found through the path of self-discovery and self-surrender to God.

* * *

[Jesus] said, "Who touched my clothes?" . . . The woman fearing and trembling, knowing what was done in her, came and fell down before him, and told him all the truth. And he said unto her, "Daughter, thy faith hath made thee whole; go in peace, and be whole of thy plague." (Mark 5:30,33-34, KJV)

* * *

Saul dressed David in his own tunic. He put a coat of armor on him and a bronze helmet on his head. David fastened on his sword over the tunic and tried walking around, because he was not used to them.

"I cannot go in these," he said to Saul, "because I am not used to them." So he took them off. Then he took his staff in his hand, chose five smooth stones from the stream, put them in the pouch of his shepherd bag and, with his sling in his hand, approached the Philistine. (I Samuel 17:38-40, NIV)

You have defecated to block the road.
(Kaje)

✳

Many people lose opportunities in life because of their irrational or ridiculous behavior. They engage in endless nit-picking. They insist on having their way. They forget to show gratitude or to give respect. And so, as they become obsessed with self, opportunities pass them by.

Mental balance is key. Gentleness of mind is a fruit of the Spirit (Galatians 5:22) but is also an aspect of the disciple's life that we must constantly work at. Gentleness does not mean giving up discernment but it does mean letting go of our opinionated, counter-productive thought patterns. We are not likely to seek understanding about the way open to us or to others if we allow negativity to dominate—to become "defecation."

God wants us to be open to possibilities for real growth and true progress. This is a discipline worthy of one who follows Christ, whose feet are shod with the Gospel of peace.

✳   ✳   ✳

A fool takes no pleasure in understanding, but only in expressing personal opinion. (Proverbs 18:2, NRSV)

The wasp says that regular trips to a mud pit enable it to build a house.

✳

The Count of Monte Cristo is one of my favorite novels because in it faith overcomes all adversity. The book's main character, Edmond Dantes, was abused by his employer, betrayed by his friends, and falsely imprisoned by the local authorities. While being held in an island fortress, he was fortunate enough to befriend an abbé (French priest) who occupied an adjacent cell. The abbé taught him philosophy and etiquette, but most importantly, he instilled in the young Edmond some hope about the future. A great treasure lay beyond the walls of the castle. Edmond could have it if he exercised patience and presence of mind.

Edmond took on the challenge and painstakingly began to devise a strategy to break free. For several years, he chipped away at his cell wall, using a blunt instrument he had turned into a knife. He never wavered in the pursuit of his goal. Finally he escaped. He eventually found the treasure that the abbé had told him about and instantly became one of the wealthiest men of Europe.

How did he make it? On spiritual stamina—persistence. It is the stuff of faith.

*   *   *

I have fought the good fight, I have finished the race; I have kept the faith. (2 Timothy 4:7, NRSV)

A good name is better than riches.
(Ishan)

✳

One of my favorite biblical characters is Abraham. He was once called Abram. His name change accents a change in his character—a change for the better.

Abraham remains a hero for me, not simply because he *believed in* God, but because he *believed* God. As a result, he was established as the grand patriarch of the Jewish people. The writer of Hebrews says this: "By faith Abraham, when he was called to go out into a place which he should after receive for an inheritance, obeyed; and he went out not knowing whither he went" (Hebrews 11:8, KJV).

It is Abraham's name that the Judeo-Christian tradition celebrates, not his riches. Riches are fleeting. You come into the world without them, and you will leave without them. However, a person's name, when blessed, carries with it the signature of eternity. That is what Jesus said of the woman who anointed his feet with perfume. "What she has done will be told, in memory of her" (Mark 14:9, NIV).

Abraham is known for his faith, not his finances. Job is regarded for his patience and not his pecuniary fortune. Solomon had the world's wealth, yet he prayed for wisdom, not wealth, and the Lord endowed him with both. Work on building your character. Be a person of integrity, peace, and justice, and your name will provide you access to places that money cannot.

*   *   *

A good name is rather to be chosen than great riches, and loving favour rather than silver and gold. (Proverbs 22:1, KJV)

Arrogance is a sign of poverty.
(West Africa)

✳

Pharaoh was a poor man. He lacked a relationship with Jehovah. His trust was in his position and not in providence. He sneered at Moses and snubbed him. Pharaoh's pride blinded him. He consistently overlooked escape routes, opportunities to come to a peaceable solution and salvage his empire. He was a victim of spiritual deprivation, which eventually led to the political and economic collapse of his kingdom.

People who refuse wisdom are like the boxer who is in a championship fight with no corner to direct him. He is left to the mercies of his opponents, the fear, the crowd, and his diminished wits. Similarly, King Saul was disgraced in death because he sought to obtain an advantage in life by appealing to a source other than God. Arrogance is a short path to the deep pit of condemnation. Love is its only cure.

* * *

If I have prophetic powers, and understand all mysteries and all knowledge, and if I have all faith, so as to remove mountains, but do not have love, I am nothing. (I Corinthians 13:2, NRSV)

16

Because friendship is pleasant,
we partake of our friend's entertainment, not because we
have not enough to eat in our own house.
(West Africa)

✳

There is a thin line between love and hate. There is a thinner line between familiarity and contempt. How often do we hear of abuse? We are created for relationship, yet ego, power, and greed obscure our capacity to see others in a loving way.

We dishonor God when we dishonor human relationships and friendships. When God sends people to us to receive something, God desires blessings for all involved. People seek your company because they feel that they will be treated with respect and dignity (that is, they feel that their souls will be enhanced by your company); however, they are not desperate. Do not assume that people cannot go on without you. Only fools will leave the warmth and pleasantness of their homes to be abused.

Shallow people often make the mistake of thinking that people want something from them. People who do this soon find that they have few friends. People come to you to be affirmed, not abused. They come to be blessed, not belittled. Be prepared to be a blessing in season and out of season.

* * *

The natives showed us unusual kindness. Since it had begun to rain and was cold, they kindled a fire and welcomed all of us around it. (Acts 28:2, NRSV)

* * *

Do nothing from selfish ambition or conceit, but in humility regard others as better than yourselves. (Philippians 2:3, NRSV)

PART TWO

"What Goes Around
Comes Around":

The Moral Law

If the eye can endure smoke, it will see fire.
(Nupe)

*

Maria Stewart was America's first black female political writer. She was a woman of the cloth who conquered innumerable obstacles en route to her success in fighting for justice and equality for women and blacks. She did this in the early part of the nineteenth century, when it was deemed improper for women to be visible political figures and when many African Americans were still held in chains. Stewart defended herself by appealing to Scripture and by defining herself as a servant of Christ. She is quoted in *Maria Stewart: America's First Black Woman Political Writer* (Indiana University Press, 1987): "The Spirit of God came before me and I spake before many . . . reflecting on what I had said, I felt ashamed. . . . something said within my breast, 'Press forwards, I will be with thee.' And my heart made this reply, 'Lord, if thou wilt be with me, then I will speak for thee as long as I live.'"

Because Maria Stewart endured the smoke of alienation, oppression, and ignorance, she was able to see the fire of success in her political campaign for justice.

* * *

Therefore take up the whole armor of God, so that you may be able to withstand on that evil day, and having done everything, to stand firm. (Ephesians 6:13, NRSV)

No matter how long the night, the day is sure to come.
(Zaire)

✳

African American experience is a portrait of tears of triumph and cries of celebration. It is an experience of beauty that has turned to ashes and back again to beauty. In a lecture entitled "A Charge To Keep," Dr. Calvin Butts, pastor of the Abyssinian Baptist Church of Harlem, New York, describes the African American struggle of faith, saying, "Our faith is a recital of deeds actually recorded in the real stuff of history. God did something for us. We saw God part the Red Sea. We saw him raise Lazarus from the dead. Yes, manna has fallen from heaven." James Weldon Johnson's classic words bring beauty to this story of the struggle:

*   *   *

Stony the road we trod,
Bitter the chastening rod,
Felt in the days when hope unborn had died;
Yet with a steady beat,
Have not our weary feet
Come to the place for which our fathers sighed?
We have come over a way that with tears have been watered,
We have come, treading our path through the blood of the slaughtered,
Out from the gloomy past,
Till now we stand at last
Where the white gleam of our bright star is cast.

—James Weldon Johnson

*   *   *

Weeping may endure for a night, but joy cometh in the morning. (Psalm 30:5, KJV)

You don't miss your water till your well runs dry.
(West Africa)

❋

What is the common thread that binds all the biblical prophets together? Hosea, Jeremiah, Isaiah, and Micah all preached one sermon with many variations: "Return to God before it's too late."

Are you frittering away your time, your talents, your resources, your relationship with God?

It may appear that your water will never run out, because water is abundant. At the same time, it *is* a valuable substance. Though nearly seventy percent of the earth's surface is water, we often overlook its great significance. Likewise, we often overlook the good things we have until it is too late and they are long gone. Make a concerted attempt to recognize those persons and possessions that are crucial to your well-being and success and give them credit. Be diligent in acknowledging the virtues and the work of others.

*   *   *

O God, you are my God, I seek you, my soul thirsts for you; my flesh faints for you, as in a dry and weary land where there is no water. (Psalm 63:1, NRSV)

A child is better than riches.
(Ishan)

✳

Children have memories; riches lack memories. The love of children is the root of family; the love of riches is the root of all evil. Children bring joy and responsibility; riches bring enemies and a lot of heartache.

God is concerned about children. There is no record of Jesus telling the disciples to "suffer the rich to come unto me." Hence, those who invest in children are closer to God spiritually. People's riches and loyalty must be in the kingdom to make life better. Riches do not make life; children do. The Igbos of Nigeria have a saying: "The human being answers; wealth does not."

Children tie us to God because they show us how utterly fragile and dependent we are. We need others. We need fellowship. To understand this is to make strides toward true spiritual maturity—a closer walk with God.

* * *

"Truly I tell you, unless you change and become like children, you will never enter the kingdom of heaven." (Matthew 18:3, NRSV)

If your hair is not as long as your friend's, do not plait it like hers.
(Nupe)

✳

"Imitation is suicide," wrote Ralph Waldo Emerson. God is not into mass production. Neither does God like to suffocate creative spirits. Rather, God has a peculiar and particular blueprint for each soul. This is what it means to be created in God's image and likeness.

Let us learn from others. Let us not ape them. Our identity, our individual creativity should never be subsumed under another's, for this is tantamount to soul murder. This is why freedom accompanies grace as a gift of faith. The more we allow ourselves to be guided and empowered by the Spirit, the more we experience the freedom to create. We no longer have to submit to slavery. Christ has set us free.

Dr. King used to caution his hearers to be the best of whoever they were. A wise person once said, "Do not follow where the path may lead. Go instead where there is no path and leave a trail."

＊　＊　＊

When you turn to the right or when you turn to the left, your ears shall hear a word behind you, saying, "This is the way; walk in it." (Isaiah 30:21, NRSV)

A deer with a long neck tends to get hit by a stray bullet.
(Setswana)

Curiosity is the seed of genius. Genius, however, is curiosity disciplined.

The capacity to discover is built into our psychological makeup. Every significant achievement of humankind finds its origins in the seed of curiosity. However, curiosity, like food, can be used for good or evil. When it is used for good, it is dubbed something attractive, like innovation or perception. When it is used recklessly, it is called a host of negative things.

To become unwittingly involved with the affairs of others is like walking the plank—it is a slow form of social suicide. Does not the day carry with it sufficient problems for itself? Is life not complicated enough? Why intensify your headaches by piling on other people's problems? Our communities are filled with people who carry the luggage of others. That is why we are commanded in the Scriptures to lay our burdens down (Matthew 11:28-30).

Remember also that those who meddle are often hit by stray bullets. When you meddle, you open yourself to abuse and insult that you can well do without. Self-respect, independent thinking, and confidentiality are key virtues of Christian character.

* * *

Those who guard their mouths preserve their lives;
those who open wide their lips come to ruin. (Proverbs 13:3, NRSV)

* * *

Like one who seizes a dog by the ears
    is a passer-by who meddles in a quarrel not his own.
Like a madman shooting
    firebrands or deadly arrows
is a man who deceives his neighbor. (Proverbs 26:17-19, NIV)

You cannot hide the smoke of the hut you set on fire.
(Burundi)

✳

Ev•i•dence. n. 1. Ground for belief; that which tends to prove or disprove something; proof. 2. The manifestation of an act committed or a word uttered. **Con•se•quence.** n. 1. Act or fact of following as an effect or result upon something antecedent.

All actions leave behind some evidence. Consequences follow past actions, wise or foolish. Are you considering getting married, having children, starting on a new career path, taking a radical position on some issue? Before you make a serious, life-changing decision, weigh your alternatives. Pray. Seek counsel.

There are some choices about which it is worth seeking advice. For this reason the book of Proverbs states,

A wise man has great power,
and a man of knowledge increases strength;
for waging war you need guidance,
and for victory many advisers. (Proverbs 24:5-6, NIV)

Foolish actions always beget disastrous consequences. A person cannot expect to commit an act without facing the results. Furthermore, it is difficult to cover a catastrophe, to make up for lost time, or to close the door of the barn after the horses have escaped. So be cautious. As Ben Franklin put it, an ounce of prevention is worth a pound of cure. Take lessons from the book of foresight.

*   *   *

Keep your conscience clear, so that, when you are maligned, those who abuse you for your good conduct in Christ may be put to shame. (1 Peter 3:16, NRSV)

People start preparing for the night when the day is still very young.
(Igala)

✳

Those who would live full lives recognize that time is precious. The time we have been given is a gift from God, not to be squandered. Even in the "down moments" of life we can prepare ourselves for more crucial times.

And when those times come, we need to be ready to take action. Christ said, "Zacchaeus, make haste, and come down" (Luke 19:5, KJV). Zacchaeus did not hesitate. Immediately, at the call of Christ, he came down from the tree.

What if he had said, "I will wait until the crowd leaves, when I am out of the public eye" or "Let me check his social references and hear what other people have to say about him"? If Zacchaeus had hesitated, he would never have found Christ. This was his first and only chance to meet the Savior. Never again would Jesus pass through Jericho; it was now or never.

Many of us face times in life when we must make quick and firm decisions. Will we be able to make the right decision? We will be better equipped to do so if we prepare while the day is still young.

* * *

For with you is the fountain of life; in your light we see light. (Psalm 36:9, NRSV)

* * *

"Be dressed for action and have your lamps lit; be like those who are waiting for their master to return from the wedding banquet, that they may open the door for him as soon as he comes and knocks." (Luke 12:35-36, NRSV)

Whose mother is at the pot will not lack soup.
(Bwatiye)

✳

Mom smiles at obstacles. She can pull a gourmet meal out of last night's left-overs. She runs an international organization on a shoestring budget. She is like the Energizer bunny: She "just keeps on going and going and going." I don't have to look for a moral exemplar, because she is one.

What is motherhood? Resilience, industry, creativity, courage, patience, the ability to envision the future and to prepare children for its challenges. All of the above and a whole lot of grace. Any woman who takes the time to do these things is necessarily a leader, a visionary, and a virtuous person. These qualities are primary ingredients for developing children who grow up to be gifts to the world.

Read Hannah's prayer to God in 1 Samuel 1. It contains the seeds of radical obedience. Also consider Mary, the mother of Jesus. Her life is a transcendent testimony. One thing can be said about these women: their eyes were watching God.

Thanks, Mom.

* * *

[Elijah] said, "Go outside, borrow vessels from all your neighbors, empty vessels and not just a few. Then go in, and shut the door behind you and your children, and start pouring into all these vessels; when each is full, set it aside." So she left him and shut the door behind her and her children; they kept bringing vessels to her, and she kept pouring. When the vessels were full, she said to her son, "Bring me another vessel." But he said to her, "There are no more." Then the oil stopped flowing. She came and told the man of God, and he said, "Go sell the oil and pay your debts, and you and your children can live on the rest." (2 Kings 4:3-7, NRSV)

26

Lice do not grow on a bald head.
(Yoruba)

✳

Humility is a book written in three chapters: "Have reverence for God," "Have regard for others," and "Have respect for self."

To be humble means to devote oneself to the program of providence, which is to love all of God's children. It does not mean weakness or timidity. The renowned ethicist Katie Canon called it "unshouted joy." Those who remain open, clear, and true to themselves are God's most trusted servants, for they understand the gift of integrity. They are the stewards who go and invest their talents and are able to offer the master a good return on his investment. Those who lack humility often suffer self-deception and are thus easily deceived by others.

It is hard to corrupt a humble spirit, for such a person constantly engages in acts of self-surrender and self-purification. The humble are directed by the spirit of truth and defended by the great Advocate, the Spirit. Remain humble and you will have fewer headaches (lice).

* * *

When pride comes, then comes disgrace;
  but wisdom is with the humble. (Proverbs 11:2, NRSV)

* * *

All of you, clothe yourselves with humility toward one another, because,
  "God opposes the proud
    but gives grace to the humble."
Humble yourselves, therefore, under God's mighty hand, that he may lift you up in due time. Cast all your anxiety upon him because he cares for you. (I Peter 5:5-7, NIV)

Do not call the forest that shelters you a jungle.
(West Africa)

※

Insults hurt. They pierce deeply. To be insulted by those to whom you have shown care and concern hurts even more.

Remember Judas. He hurt the one who loved him more than anyone else in the world. He destroyed his own spiritual home, his source of power.

You and I may not be that callous. However, we partake in other activities that weaken our wisdom and our witness, our mission and our message. And by so doing we insult our faith heritage: the church. Condescending criticism, malicious gossip, a contemptuous look, and chronic, corrosive bitterness only destroy our community of faith.

Count your blessings. Ingratitude has a way of coming back to haunt the person who shows it. Moreover, if you destroy that which houses you, you will soon be left without protection, preservation, or provision.

Nurture your environment. Enhance those who are around you. Make the situation better; do not tear it down by sharp, critical, or unkind words. Let us deny the Judas in us and affirm the Jesus within us.

* * *

You have no excuse, whoever you are, when you judge others; for in passing judgment on another you condemn yourself, because you, the judge, are doing the very same things. (Romans 2:1, NRSV)

* * *

Do not speak evil against one another, brothers and sisters. Whoever speaks evil against another or judges another, speaks evil against the law and judges the law; but if you judge the law, you are not a doer of the law but a judge. (James 4:11, NRSV)

One who eats corruption will die corrupted.
(Yoruba)

✳

Thoughts are to the mind as blood is to the body. Your thoughts have power. They are capable of driving people toward you or driving people away from you.

"Let all bitterness and wrath and anger and clamor and slander be put away from you, along with all malice. Be kind to one another, tender-hearted, forgiving each other, just as God in Christ also has forgiven you" (Ephesians 4:31-32, NASB). Eliminate any words of bitterness from your mental conversation. Give your mind positive food.

Be more like David who strengthened himself in the Lord. The Psalms are exercises in psychological and spiritual empowerment that teach and encourage us to rise above our own hurts. Through these felt experiences of others, we grow stronger, too.

* * *

Finally, beloved, whatever is true, whatever is honorable, whatever is just, whatever is pure, whatever is pleasing, whatever is commendable, if there is any excellence and if there is anything worthy of praise, think about these things. (Philippians 4:8, NRSV)

The child looks everywhere
but does not know what to look for.
The old man looks for one thing and sees everything.
(Senegal)

✳

The child has not yet found God and thus lacks the lens through which to understand the vicissitudes of life. The elderly man focuses his spiritual gaze upon one subject—God, the one who lays the foundation of the universe, the author and finisher of all knowledge. When we are forgetful of God, we too, like a child, lose focus and are drawn by anything that captures our attention. But it may only hold our interest momentarily, because it is not the heart of the matter, and we could go on searching forever, and *unknowingly*.

When we look for the one thing that matters, the Lord of all, everything comes into focus. Our spiritual eyes are enlightened and our hearts comprehend what our minds cannot fully grasp. We regain our vision by seeking God who sees and knows our need for a truer lens, a faithful Lord and a better heart.

*   *   *

Those who know your name put their trust in you, for you, O LORD, have not forsaken those who seek you. (Psalm 9:10, NRSV)

*   *   *

One thing I do: Forgetting what is behind and straining toward what is ahead, I press on toward the goal to win the prize for which God has called me heavenward in Christ Jesus. (Philippians 3:13-14, NIV)

Lack of knowledge made the hen to sleep on a bundle of corn.
(Angas People)

✳

Misuse and abuse squash talent. Like the hen that did not realize what wealth of nourishment she dozed upon, we too waste away our opportunities and resources. Even many who saw Jesus' life suffered such a fate: They realized too late who he was.

Gifts come and go. In their season, they seem inexhaustible, and then, in a whiff, they are gone. There is a time for everything under the sun. The season of feasting is closely followed by the season of famine. And how well one does during feasting season shapes how well one is equipped to endure famine. I have heard older folk say, "You don't miss your water till your well runs dry."

It is imperative to use one's time and resources wisely. Fortunately, the means are available for us to make a gourmet meal from raw material: Make use of the seasoning of prayer and fasting. Turn up the fire of passion. Apply the pepper of discipline. Do not take your meal until preparation is complete. Consult the taste buds of others. Share. Take correction and advice from friends, teachers, and elders. Do not consume too much. Save some leftovers for the season of famine.

* * *

"Who then is the faithful and wise slave, whom his master has put in charge of his household, to give the other slaves their allowance of food at the proper time? Blessed is that slave whom his master will find at work when he arrives. Truly I tell you, he will put that one in charge of all his possessions." (Matthew 25:45-47, NRSV)

**To his hosts, the incoming stranger first appeared like gold,
then turned to silver, and eventually ended up as crude iron.**
(Ethiopia)

✳

In the first months of courtship, people see in their beloveds what they want to see. Only after that initial period do they see other things. We all play our various roles on the stage of the world. We play certain parts and appear in certain disguises. Yet, this is a double-edged sword. For if we do this, then we present disguises to the world and we also see the world through our disguises. Both our act and our perception involves at least to some degree the falsification or alteration of reality. And perhaps this is why it is often said that truth is a bitter pill to swallow. Not only because we feel other people may have deceived us, but because we also have deceived ourselves.

Perhaps this is why Jesus touched the blind man twice. The first time, the man regaining his sight saw men as trees walking. Obtaining clear vision is a process. It requires growth, a constant struggle. The man required a second touch in order to see men as men and trees as trees. First comes the clearing of whatever prevents us from seeing from the inside out, and then comes the ability to discern between gold and silver and iron.

*   *   *

They came to Bethsaida, and some people brought a blind man and begged Jesus to touch him. He took the blind man by the hand and led him outside the village. When he had spit on the man's eyes and put his hands on him, Jesus asked, "Do you see anything?" He looked up and said, "I see people; they look like trees walking around." Once more Jesus put his hands on the man's eyes. Then his eyes were opened, his sight was restored, and he saw everything clearly. (Mark 8:22-25, NIV)

Seeing or spotting an animal in the bush or hunting ground is not tantamount to shooting and killing it.

(Cameroon)

✳

Lots of people can spot a problem. Others can spot solutions. But at the end of the day, ideas do not pay bills. A dream unfulfilled is at best a fantasy and at worst frustration. Human eyes can easily spot an animal on a hunting ground or in the forest. But seeing is one thing; killing is another.

This is stubbornly true with Christianity. One can be a theological and biblical genius and yet be alien to salvation. One can be smart but not saved. Theological and biblical expertise is not enough. The missing piece is faith in Jesus Christ. Knowledge about faith might be present, but again, this is not enough. Faith and works must work hand in glove. It is not just knowing but *knowing and doing* that makes a difference.

* * *

You must make every effort to support your faith with goodness, and goodness with knowledge, and knowledge with self-control, and self-control with endurance, and endurance with godliness, and godliness with mutual affection, and mutual affection with love. For if these things are yours and are increasing among you, they keep you from being ineffective and unfruitful in the knowledge of our Lord Jesus Christ. (I Peter I:5-8, NRSV)

PART THREE

"Tell It Like It Is":

Human Nature

His opinions are like water in the bottom of a canoe, going from side to side.

✳

Politicians are known to waver. So are Christians. We talk a good game, but it's easier to say what we do than to do what we say. That is why trustworthy people are hard to come by.

The problem is that most of us do not trust ourselves. We make decisions based more on feeling than on faith. Our shoddiness of character often springs from a lack of moral training or a deep insecurity concerning our identity (or both). Hence, we stand as candidates for betrayal, carrying with us the virus of envy and jealousy. We end up devoid of courage to stand on the side of truth, even when the truth will help us.

We must stand on the side of truth. The truth sets us free.

*   *   *

The doubter, being double-minded and unstable in every way, must not expect to receive anything from the Lord. (James 1:8, NRSV)

*   *   *

A simple man believes anything,
but a prudent man gives thought to his steps. (Proverbs 14:15, NIV)

*   *   *

A man who strays from the path of understanding
comes to rest in the company of the dead. (Proverbs 21:16, NIV)

*   *   *

Let us hold fast to the confession of our hope without wavering, for he who has promised is faithful. (Hebrews 10:23, NRSV)

No matter how long a log stays in water, it does not become a crocodile.
(West Africa)

✳

Is change inevitable? I'm not so sure anymore. Some things and some people are simply the way they are. Habits formed early on typically set in and become cemented. The conditions may be altered, but character often remains constant.

Do not spend endless hours trying to change people. Change of this sort is a voluntary act that can proceed only from the heart. Remember that the prodigal son could not help himself until he "came to himself" (Luke 15:17). What transforms a thing comes from the inside and not the outside. This is good news, because an interior work of the Holy Spirit is lasting change. Not only does a work of grace—from the inside out—happen, it happens deeply. It gets at the truth both about us and about God. God wants more for us than we want for ourselves.

*   *   *

"If you hold to my teaching, you are really my disciples. Then you will know the truth, and the truth will set you free." (John 8:31-32, NIV)

We work on the surface. The depths are a mystery.
(Bahaya)

✳

The great developments in science have not been matched by equal achievements in human fellowship and peace. Why is the human family so technically proficient but so morally deficient? It seems we have great knowledge when it comes to making life easy but very little when it comes to the ultimate meaning of existence. The ultimate purpose of life is a mystery to us. God alone supplies the answers. Take a leaf from the notebook of a moral genius, Martin Luther King Jr., in *Where Do We Go From Here: Chaos or Community?*

> The real problem is with man himself and man's soul. We haven't learned how to be just and honest and kind and true and loving…. The real problem is that with our scientific genius we've made of the world a neighborhood, but through our moral and spiritual genius we've failed to make it a brotherhood. And the great danger facing us today is not so much the atomic bomb that was created by physical science … but the real problem lies in the hearts and souls of men capable of exploding into the vilest hate and into the most damaging selfishness— that's the problem we've got to fear today.

Sounds like Dr. King was a true prophet.

* * *

For we do not proclaim ourselves; we proclaim Jesus Christ as Lord and ourselves as your slaves for Jesus' sake. For it is the God who said, "Let light shine out of darkness," who has shone in our hearts to give the light of the knowledge of the glory of God in the face of Jesus Christ. But we have this treasure in clay jars, so that it may be clear that this extraordinary power belongs to God and does not come from us. (2 Corinthians 4:5-7, NRSV)

Whoever goes after two termite hills returns empty-handed.
(Bahaya)

✳

Ambition is a good thing—to a point. It must be anointed. If left unchecked, it becomes exploitative.

The Scriptures are replete with the works of people who had anointed ambition and providential purpose. Abraham had to go to another land in order to fulfill his destiny. Moses was an underachiever until he trusted God. David's greatness came on the heels of holy passion. Jesus even told his disciples, "The one who believes in me will also do the works that I do and, in fact, will do greater works than these" (John 14:12, NRSV).

Remember these words: "If you have faith the size of a mustard seed, you will say to this mountain, 'Move from here to there,' and it will move" (Matthew 17:20, NRSV). There is one requirement for this kind of greatness: one's steps must be ordered by the Lord. You cannot bear too many burdens and expect to be a whole human being. A wise person once said, "A man's got to know his limitations." Lack of focus brings failure. Too many programs bequeath too many problems. Seek the one thing God has put you on this earth to do, and do that with all your might.

* * *

The plans of the diligent lead surely to abundance,
   but everyone who is hasty comes only to want. (Proverbs 21:5, NRSV)

A bird is in the air, but its mind is on the ground.
(Mandinka)

✳

We may see the Christian life as so freeing that it would seem we should be like a bird on a wing for most of the time. The Apostle Paul speaks of being at liberty to do anything he pleases, because he is confident that he will not be mastered by anything (1 Corinthians 6:12, NRSV). True consecration results in a disciple of Jesus being free to follow in the way of truth and life. God's direction is for us to go a grounded route, a humble way of reaching the heights as a result of first making our faith count in modest faithfulness.

Fred Craddock, Professor of Homiletics at Emory University, caught the practical implications of consecration in an address he gave to aspiring ministers. "To give my life for Christ appears glorious," he said. "To pour myself out for others … to pay the ultimate price of martyrdom—I'll do it. I'm ready, Lord, to go out in a blaze of glory. We think giving our all to the Lord is like taking $1,000.00 bill and laying it on the table—'Here's my life, Lord. I'm giving it all.' But the reality for most of us is that he sends us to the bank and has us cash in the $1,000.00 for quarters. We go through life putting out 25 cents here and 50 cents there. Listen to the neighbor kid's troubles instead of saying, 'Get lost.' Go to a committee meeting. Give a cup of water to a shaky old man in a nursing home. Usually giving our life to Christ isn't glorious. It's done in all those little acts of love, 25 cents at time. It would be easy to go out in a flash of glory; it's harder to live the Christian life little by little over the long haul."

*   *   *

He has told you, O mortal, what is good; and what does the LORD require of you but to do justice, and to love kindness, and to walk humbly with your God? (Micah 6:8, NRSV)

When the cock is drunk, he forgets about the hawk.
(Ashanti)

✳

Moderation. It is easier to spell or to say than to practice.

Moderation is essential to ministry. However, evil seeks to ambush both. Evil makes us drunk on the cares of this world, our desires, our work. It begins by providing relief, however fleeting. It then moves in ambitiously for the kill. Its effects are devastating. Like overindulgence in alcohol, evil dulls the senses, suspends intelligence, and impairs the ability to see clearly, choking off our spiritual integrity.

As Dietrich Bonhoeffer said, nothing must come between the believer and Christ. Not fame, not fortune, not even ministry or personal piety. Our devotion must be to Christ alone. Jesus said, "Take heed, watch and pray for you do not know when the time is [of his return]" (Mark 13:32, NKJV). And Paul wrote to the Ephesians, "Do not be drunk with wine, in which is dissipation; but be filled with the Spirit" (Ephesians 5:18, NKJV).

In our hedonistic society, many in the church have become drunk on the wine of "thingism." We buy things in order to address inner spiritual problems, thinking that having more stuff will cure us. Yet material things can at best provide only temporary relief for spiritual needs.

Materialism is an intoxicant. It draws us away from reality by drawing our focus to the fleeting and finite while ignoring the root cause of the evil that affects our souls, families, and communities. My advice: stay alive. Pray in season and out of season.

*   *   *

He who loves pleasure will become poor;
  whoever loves wine and oil will never be rich. (Proverbs 21:17, NIV)

The heart of man and the bottom of the sea are unfathomable.
(West Africa)

✳

Ever tried mind reading? How about soul reading? Difficult! Dodgy! Try humanly impossible!

To be obsessed with the contents of another's mind is a thankless task. It creates spiritual restlessness, mistrust, doubt, and defeatism (that is, mental poison). Such work is slow but steady suicide. But behold! To be obsessed with the mind of God leads to life, love, and learning.

How do we learn God's mind? By reading God's Word. As one songwriter said, "Keep my steps steady according to your promise" (Psalm 119:133, NRSV). Nothing relieves and ventilates the mind like a firm commitment to God's unwavering Word.

* * *

Trust in the Lord with all thine heart. . . . In all thy ways acknowledge him, and he shall direct thy paths. (Proverbs 3:5-6, KJV)

* * *

If any of you is lacking in wisdom, ask God, who gives to all generously and ungrudgingly, and it will be given you. But ask in faith, never doubting, for the one who doubts is like a wave of the sea, driven and tossed by the wind; for the doubter, being double-minded and unstable in every way, must not expect to receive anything from the Lord. (James 1:5-8, NRSV)

Hunter in pursuit of an elephant
does not stop to throw stones at birds.
(Uganda)

＊

Detractors come and go, but anything worth pursuing has lasting value. When Nehemiah rallied the people of Israel to rebuild the wall around Jerusalem and remove the disgrace of his people, he was met with taunts, jeers, and intimidating letters from the provincial governors. Nehemiah replied as a man in pursuit of an elephant: "The God of heaven is the one who will give us success, and we his servants are going to start building" (Nehemiah 2:20, NRSV).

Martin Luther King Jr. wrote his celebrated "Letter from Birmingham Jail" (April 16, 1963) in response to criticism by eight of the city's leading white clergymen that King's strategies were extreme and illegal. King responded with eloquence, cogency, and simplicity. He seized upon an opportunity to reveal to the world the integrity, morality, and meaningfulness of the Civil Rights Movement. King's sights were fixed on the elephant.

> My Dear Fellow Clergymen: While confined here in the Birmingham city jail, I came across your recent statement calling my present activities "unwise and untimely." Seldom do I pause to answer criticism of my work and ideas…. But since I feel that you are men of genuine good will and that your criticisms are sincerely set forth, I want to try to answer your statements in what I hope will be patient and reasonable terms.

＊   ＊   ＊

Because the Sovereign LORD helps me, I will not be disgraced. Therefore have I set my face like flint, and I know I will not be put to shame. He who vindicates me is near. Who then will bring charges against me? Let us face each other! Who is my accuser? Let him confront me! (Isaiah 50:7-8, NRSV)

It is an egg that becomes a cock.
(Yoruba)

✳

When you view the world and its diversity, do you see a mere person or do you see God at work making something marvelous? How do you treat small children, young people in general? Have you ever stopped to think that you might be in the presence of tomorrow's great personalities?

Below are the names of some weighty achievers who began as eggs, full of potential. They were not always recognized or appreciated. They spent many years being invisible. They endured being overlooked, ignored, snubbed and slighted. Yet, they had nascent greatness. Many people simply refused to look deeply enough to find it.

Toni Morrison. Literary genius, Nobel Prize winner in literature; she overcame divorce and a fire that burnt her home to ashes.

Michael Jordan. Six-time world champion basketball player; he was cut from his high school basketball team and endured the death of his father.

Nelson Mandela. Ambassador for global peace; he was imprisoned for over 25 years by the South African apartheid government.

Muhammad Ali. Three-time heavyweight champion of the world; he was publicly ridiculed and scorned, and stripped of his heavyweight title.

✳ ✳ ✳

I am confident of this, that the one who began a good work among you will bring it to completion by the day of Jesus Christ. (Philippians 1:6, NRSV)

Tiger does not have to proclaim its Tigritude.
(Wole Soyinka, Nigeria)

✳

Freedom is a gift. It gives us the capacity for self-transcendence. We can survey our condition and transform it. Yet we must remember that we are also part of the animal kingdom, citizens in realm of fauna and flaura. So, we are free and yet bound, creative yet constricted, imaginative yet insecure. We are human. Thus we partake in poetry, philosophy, preaching, tent-making, marriage, funerals, and various other religious and cultural rituals.

The natural world is a vast and vital theatre of knowledge, a dynamic classroom of human learning and expansion. Because we are creaturely, we suffer a certain kind of anxiety. This anxiety accents a deep insecurity and causes us to overcompensate by overstepping our boundaries. Often this insecurity is expressed through intimidation or aggression toward others. We mask an inferiority complex in acts of superiority.

A tiger never does this. That willful act would reduce its tigerliness (tigritude). When people boast recklessly, the world wonders if they are truly great. The truly strong do not need to convince others of their strength. That is why the Bura people say, "A person does not carry his land on his head."

*   *   *

God chose what is low and despised in the world, things that are not, to reduce to nothing things that are, so that no one might boast in the presence of God. He is the source of your life in Christ Jesus, who became for us wisdom from God, and righteousness and sanctification and redemption, in order that, as it is written, "Let the one who boasts, boast in (I) the Lord."
(I Corinthians I:28-3I, NRSV)

43

When two brothers fight,
strangers always reap the harvest.
(Igbo)

✳

When Barry Bonds hit his major league record-breaking home run, the world roared in jubilation. Newspapers plastered it on the front page, radio stations changed their morning programs, and sportscasters sent out a dizzying array of buzzwords and word-pictures to describe the unforgettable feat—a milestone for Barry Bonds.

Not everyone joined in. At least two people opted out. Who? Two fans fought over who was the rightful owner of the ball that Bonds hit to break the record. The debate raged in the media. Each party hired a lawyer who took the case to court. It was a bitter, nasty, draining affair. The verdict: Both men were given equal rights to the ball. But there was one problem. They had to pay their respective lawyers.

In a moment the two men went from victors to victims. After the sale of the baseball, they were left holding the bag. Almost every cent was paid out in legal fees, and we are left to wonder: If they had come to a peaceable agreement way before the situation had gone sour, how would they have benefited? Surely they would have reaped a reward instead of the lawyers. Peace produces prosperity. Egoism only begets enmity.

* * *

How very good and pleasant it is when kindred live together in unity! (Psalm 133:1, NRSV)

PART FOUR

"Walk Together, Children":

Collective Responsibility and Cooperative Ethics

Streams make up a river.
(Buji)

＊

"A self-made man?" the preacher thundered. "A self-made man?" he repeated quizzically. "I pray I never meet such a creature. I have a hard enough time dealing with persons who were made by two people." The point was bold yet subtle. The audience roared.

That the ego-driven person always fizzles out is clear from the weekly tabloids. Pride typically precedes failure. No matter how brilliant, how talented, how mentally tough, a person can hardly be self-made. Any noteworthy individual has been nourished by the teaching, guidance, correction, and encouragement of others. Cooperation is the mother of commitment. That is why it is said in Ghana, "One finger does not lift a pot."

* * *

According to the grace of God given to me, like a skilled master builder I laid a foundation, and someone else is building on it. Each builder must choose with care how to build on it. (I Corinthians 3:10, NRSV)

If you have a stick, no one will bite you.

✳

How does one survive? This is Derrick Bell's response:

> If we are to extract solutions from the lessons of the slaves' survival, and our own, we must first face squarely the unbearable landscape and climate of that survival. We yearn that our civil rights work will be crowned with success, but what we really want—want even more than success—is meaning. "Meaningfulness," as the Stanford psychiatrist Dr. Irvin Tyalom tell us, "is a by-product of engagement and commitment." This commitment and engagement is what black people have had to do since slavery: making something out of nothing. A carving out a humanity for oneself with absolutely nothing to help save imagination, will, and unbelievable strength and courage. Beating the odds while firmly believing, knowing as only they could know, the fact that the odds are stacked against them.[1]

What is the stick of moral struggle? Faith, imagination, obedience, courage, and truth. Carry your stick.

*   *   *

"Sanctify them by the truth; your word is truth." (John 17:17, NIV)

*   *   *

Brothers, whatever is true, whatever is noble, whatever is right, whatever is pure, whatever is lovely, whatever is admirable—if anything is excellent or praiseworthy—think about such things. Whatever you have learned or received or heard from me, or seen in me—put it into practice. And the God of peace will be with you. (Philippians 4:8-9, NIV)

---

1. Quoted in Herb Boyd and Robert Allen, eds., *Brotherman: The Odyssey of Black Men in America* (New York: One World, 1995), p. 375.

The world has become food for thought.
(Igala)

✳

Some people have the capacity to turn your ears into eyes. Rev. Clarence James has that rare and unique gift. I remember him once saying, "Mays turned the world into a classroom and the classroom into the world." Rev. James was lecturing to a class of young seminarians about the virtues and vision of the late Dr. Benjamin Elijah Mays, the great teacher, preacher, and president of Morehouse College.

Human beings are given a head and a heart above anything else. How we use these gifts is largely up to us. Great minds are able to make the world accessible to others. They make the world food for thought, palatable, penetrable, and understandable. I think that the Bible calls it wisdom. Give thanks for the Clarence Jameses and Benjamin Mayses in your life.

* * *

It is the wisdom of the clever to understand where they go. (Proverbs 14:8a, NRSV)

47

The ruin of a nation begins in the homes of its people.
(West Africa)

✳

Howard Thurman said, "It is the family that gives us a deep private sense of belonging. Here we first begin to have our self defined for us." Thurman was speaking to a fundamental moral law that permeates the universe. His ethico-sociological wisdom on the significance of the strong family is critical in the development of a community's capacity for peace, prosperity, and progress.

To abuse the family is to invite chaos, calamity, and catastrophe. Community is first learned within the family, for familial space is the first school. Hence, the first victim of moral bankruptcy is also the family. When people choose to abuse, disrespect, or disregard the dignity of those closest to them, then outsiders are at even greater risk. That is why, in Africa, the home is a sacred place. Wrongs that are committed outside are seen as even more flagrant abuses when committed within earshot of loved ones. Once this happens, the destruction of the nation is imminent.

* * *

If you are unwilling to serve the LORD, choose this day whom you will serve, whether the gods your ancestors served in the region beyond the River or the gods of the Amorites in whose land you are living; but as for me and my household, we will serve the LORD. (Joshua 24:15, NRSV)

One hand cannot lift a thatched roof.
(Hausa)

＊

Why did Jesus need disciples? He could have healed people with his own power. He did not seem to need the disciples when he faced the toughest obstacles in his life, when he was fleeing from Herod, when at twelve he was debating in the temple, when in the wilderness he was alone with the devil, when he was carrying his cross, when he was atoning for our sins at Calvary. Moreover, the disciples seemed to be a drag on Jesus' energy and time. They seemed to get in his way, were always quarrelling, jockeying for position, and doubting his words. One even sold him for a cheap sum. Why did Jesus employ this motley crew of social misfits? Any answer? Because he believed in teamwork and cooperation.

Is this not the meaning of church? Cooperation and teamwork organized by Jesus. Remember the Negro spiritual: "Walk together, children, dontcha git weary."

＊　　＊　　＊

Two are better than one, because they have a good reward for their toil. For if they fall, one will lift up the other; but woe to one who is alone and falls and does not have another to help. (Ecclesiastes 4:9-10, NRSV)

When a king has good counselors, his reign is peaceful.

✳

Leaders are gifts. But true gifts are not presented randomly. They carry purpose. They represent good intentions. The gift is meant to inspire, bless, or support another. The receiver honors the gift through proper use, management, and stewardship. Hence, gift exchange is a process, a story.

That is why some gifts are living things, beings. As a gift, the leader reveals hard truths through stories of triumph born out of tragedy. The leader bears the wisdom forged in the crucible of challenge, where creativity meets crisis head-on. Great leaders embody the moral strivings of their people. These are figures strong enough to draw insight, inspiration, and information from those they lead.

A leader is only as good as the followers he or she is blessed to develop. To leave bias and prejudice out of the decision-making process is crucial. Choose counselors based on who is willing to sacrifice for the cause or the mission set forth by God. This does not mean that there will be no disagreement or debate. It does mean, however, that the final word always belongs to the Holy Spirit. This is how to ensure that God's people will be served. Good counselors understand that all are important but no one is indispensable, and if God's will is served, all will be blessed. This is the meaning of peace.

* * *

Pharaoh said to Joseph, "I have had a dream, and there is no one who can interpret it. I have heard it said of you that when you hear a dream you can interpret it." Joseph answered Pharaoh, "It is not I; God will give Pharaoh a favorable answer." (Genesis 41:15-16, NRSV)

* * *

A throne is established through righteousness. (Proverbs 16:12, NIV)

It is easier to transport an anthill
than to exercise authority in the village.
(West Africa)

✳

"You have always had the handle; now you have the blade. Use it wisely," quipped Horace Orlando Russell, senior professor, to a junior member of faculty at Eastern Baptist Theological Seminary. For those who want leadership, beware. What appears to be golden and glorified is not always the substance of things hoped for. Many individuals have desired to be where successful people are, yet they are unwilling to sacrifice or to be humble enough to handle the great responsibilities.

True leadership comes with the ability to address people's needs with intelligence, patience, and humility. That is why Jesus' desire was for his disciples to be servants first. The reward of leadership can be likened unto the dessert that comes after the meal, not the hard work required to purchase groceries, prepare the meal, and set the table.

Do not pray for power. Pray, rather, for the ability to be a servant and to endure the storms of life. The old folk did not pray for an easy life but for strength to overcome life's hardships. Solomon asked God for wisdom to guide his people, not for the spoils of office. Power does not come from position but from the love God has put into broken hearts.

* * *

"The Son of Man came not to be served but to serve, and to give his life a ransom for many." (Matthew 20:28, NRSV)

Big fruits fall under big trees.
(Tangale)

✳

Association breeds attitude. Teamwork bequeaths triumph.

The 1998 Chicago Bulls won their sixth NBA title of the 1990s. At the beginning of the 1998 season, however, this team was in shambles. Michael Jordan was still "his Airness," but the rest of the Bulls looked like they were out to lunch. Some wanted more media time. Others wanted more playing time. And the supporting cast looked feeble under the pressure.

Then the team wiped away the cobwebs of doubt and ego and rallied in the play-offs. How did that happen? They achieved a careful balance of talent and tenacity. They acted as if they needed each other. A spirit of winning pervaded the entire organization. At the center of this stride toward triumph was the incomparable Coach Phil Jackson. He got the players to abandon their egos and personal goals in order to focus on one thing—winning the NBA championship. How big was Coach Phil's impact? Try this. Jordan declared earlier in the season that he would not play for any other coach.

The disciples, regardless of their personal flaws, made hanging out with Jesus a chief priority (and Jesus made hanging out with them one as well). Make a serious attempt to associate with people whose sense of self is large enough to include, affirm, and enhance others. Big thinking, like the passion that gives birth to it, is contagious. The disciples were empowered because of their association with Jesus. The early church was formed as a single, unified body. The children of Israel were liberated as a corporate entity.

* * *

Jesus told his disciples, "The one who believes in me will also do the works that I do and, in fact, will do greater works than these." (John 14:12, NRSV)

Do not leave a host's house throwing mud in his well.
(Zulu)

❋

Appreciation is the cloak of the righteous. Ingratitude is the cloak of the wicked. The optimistic find joy everywhere, for it is within them. The pessimistic and the cynical find faults everywhere, for it is their trademark. Attitude is in the blood. As people think in their hearts so are they.

If a person has taken the time to help you or serve you, it is not wise to repay him or her with ingratitude. Such a response reveals a misplaced sense of entitlement that could spring from hurt or insecurity. Nevertheless, God expects that we have a healthy self-acceptance coupled with the knowledge that we are indebted to all who add to us. Ingratitude will drain away any good we receive, while gratitude will multiply our blessings—the ones we receive and the ones we have to give.

* * *

Evil will not depart from the house of one who returns evil for good. (Proverbs 17:13, NRSV)

Make no distinction in your behavior
between those of rank and the common people.
(Ptah Hotep, 2340 B.C.)

✳

We snap at the server but not the manager—and definitely not the mayor. But in God's eyes, all human beings are equal. They have equal worth and equal dignity, and they are all endowed with sacred dignity and inexorable beauty.

It's true that there are differences in talent, intelligence, and athletic ability, and we create distinctions based on popularity, power, and prestige. However, a true Christian understands that *all* are beautiful. At the same time, all have sinned and have fallen short of the glory of God. On the one hand, we must demonize no one, no matter how criminal, banal, or sinful. On the other hand, we must deify no person, place, or institution, for this is to practice the most pernicious sin: idolatry. To treat all human beings as equal is our supreme standard. To keep this critical balance is the key to the flourishing of all relationships.

* * *

"The Spirit of the Lord is upon me,
    because he has anointed me
    to preach the gospel to the poor.
He has sent me to proclaim freedom for the prisoners
    and recovery of sight for the blind,
to release the oppressed,
    to proclaim the year of the Lord's favor." (Luke 4:18-22, NIV)

* * *

When Jesus landed and saw a large crowd, he had compassion on them, because they were like sheep without a shepherd. So he began teaching them many things. (Mark 6:34, NIV)

I am because we are.
(East Africa)

✳

Jesus was an individual, not an isolationist. His plan of human redemption came by way of collective empowerment and group advancement. He began with a motley crew of ragtag personalities whom he groomed into being world-beating disciples. These disciples formed the basis of the early church. He told Simon Peter, "On this rock I will build my church, and the gates of hell will not overcome it" (Matthew 16:18, NIV).

No doubt about it: everything we have comes from God. Yet most of the benefits of life come through human vessels. Without sound, inspiring, dedicated teachers, Dr. King would have been a mediocre sociology student. Had it not been for an unwavering, unlettered grandmother, Howard Thurman might never have become a spiritual genius. Without the support of his father, brother, and coaches, Michael Jordan might never have made it beyond the high school basketball team that cut him. Venus and Serena Williams owe their success to the unwavering dedication of their father, Richard Williams. Without the supportive commitment of their church followings, ministers such as Johnny Ray Youngblood, Floyd Flake, Kenneth Ulmer, and Bishop Vashti would not be preaching the Word.

Little wonder that the late Chief Obefemi Awolowo of Nigeria once said, "Be kind to those on your way up because you will meet them on your way down."

* * *

Remember that you were a slave in the land of Egypt, and the LORD your God brought you out from there with a mighty hand and an outstretched arm. (Deuteronomy 5:15a, NRSV)

It is because of the fact that a river flies alone that it meanders.
(Tagale)

✳

Nobody is a whole orchestra, but each musician plays a crucial part. Take away one instrument and the orchestra as a whole is weaker. Nobody is a whole team, but each member plays a role. Take away one player and the chemistry of the team is altered. No one organ makes up the whole body. But when one organ shuts down, the whole body suffers the loss.

Relationships are essential and integrating. A newborn baby would not last even a few hours without proper care. We all exist by virtue of an inescapable network of mutuality. What affects one directly affects all indirectly, as Dr. King used to remind his listeners.

It is the same in the Church. Jesus spent much time with his disciples teaching them how to build, sustain, and advance relationships. Care, concern, and commitment are essential for a church to be strong. Living a solitary existence is not only anti-biblical and unChristian, it is also deadly. In order to follow the straight and narrow path, we need to be with a family of like-minded people that helps to keep us on the straight and narrow.

*   *   *

Love each other with brotherly affection and take delight in honoring each other. Never be lazy in your work but serve the Lord enthusiastically. Be glad for all God is planning for you. Be patient in trouble, and prayerful always. When God's children are in need, you be the one to help them out. And get into the habit of inviting guests home for dinner or, if they need lodging, for the night. (Romans 12:10-13, TLB)

The shoulders are taller than the head.

✳

This proverb may be used to describe anarchic situations: when there is no balance between individuality and community; when human beings exercise more faith in their own capacities than in the work of providence; when law is recklessly discarded. However, it is most commonly used to describe a dysfunctional child-parent relationship in which parental authority has been squashed by a child's unruliness. The shoulders become taller than the head each time a Christian or the church operates on a different frequency from Jesus' own.

"A child is always a child to the parents" is a common saying in Africa. In that connection, a child is likened to the shoulders, while the parents are likened to the head. Children at the dawn of adulthood are expected to obey their parents unconditionally in the Lord. Adult children are expected to obey their parents as a mark of honor to those whom God elected to be their path of entrance into life. When a child becomes stubborn, then the shoulders are said to be taller than the head.

The call here goes to both parties. To parents: Bring up your children according to the Scriptures. To children: Obey your parents so that your days might be long in this life.

*　　*　　*

Honor your father and your mother, so that your days may be long in the land that the LORD your God is giving you. (Exodus 20:12, NRSV)

*　　*　　*

He that is of a proud heart stirreth up strife; but he that putteth his trust in the Lord shall be made whole. (Proverbs 28:25, KJV)

It is often said, "We are"; do not say, "I am."

✳

To Descartes's insight, "I think therefore I am," African traditional wisdom replies, "I am because we are." What is affirmed is a radically different moral conviction. Aggressive individuality and an obsession with pleasing the self are done away with. Selflessness and other-regard, group respect, and service to others become the norm within the community of God's people.

Strength and success would smile at the sight of "United we stand" or "Two heads are better than one." Individuality is perceived in African sociology as a mark of division, and community is seen as the abode of unity and strength. This is far from maintaining that every personal initiative or effort is wrong. Rather, the genesis of such moves should shoot out of community. It is in community that success finds abundant fertile ground and individuality is deserted.

No wonder the disciples of Jesus were always together. Little wonder the first-century missionaries were often in solidarity. Thanks be to God, early believers had everything in common and gave to each other according to their needs.

* * *

Awe came upon everyone, because many wonders and signs were being done by the apostles. All who believed were together and had all things in common; they would sell their possessions and goods and distribute the proceeds to all, as any had need. (Acts 2:43-45, NRSV)

Having a good discussion is like having riches.
(Kenya)

＊

A good discussion is give and take at its best. The wonder of it is that, rather than "evening the score," such a back-and-forth balance brings about a great multiplication of intelligence and joy.

A good discussion is neither overly subjective nor overly objective. It has the capacity to be both–and: passionate, yet clear-hearted; gracious, while truthful; yielded, but seated firmly. Personally, I love a good discussion. The gains are truly immeasurable, and therefore, they are also inestimable and inexhaustible.

One other characteristic of a good discussion is its lasting value. When people really exchange themselves by speaking together, a transaction occurs. None of the parties to the discussion is ever the same again. When faith and life in the presence of God are the main substance of a discussion, then a realm is entered where there is no end to the goodness or richness of the transaction.

In a time when we are much-assaulted with information, it is worth remembering what it means to share with other people the wealth of life experiences and stories, the treasures of faith and answered prayers we each carry with us. These have the capacity to transform others even as we have been changed through them.

＊   ＊   ＊

Then those who revered the LORD spoke with one another. The LORD took note and listened, and a book of remembrance was written before him of those who revered the LORD and thought on his name. (Malachi 3:16, NRSV)

PART FIVE

"Mold Me and Make Me":

Education and Enlightenment

Lice do not grow higher than the head.
(Used to describe rebellious children in Igal, West Africa)

✳

If misery loves company, the devil loves a crowd. Though he is defeated, on his way to oblivion, he invites others to join him at his funeral.

There is a limit to the devil's power. There are moral boundaries on evil. Dr. Johnny Ray Youngblood of the St. Paul Community Baptist Church in Brooklyn, New York, is fond of saying, "The devil may have fifteen minutes, but the divine has forty-five."

This is the faith that we live by. We have the victory in Christ Jesus. No weapon formed against us shall prosper. In fact, the weapons of the enemy only serve to make the children of God stronger. In short, God never gives us more than we can bear.

Dr. King used to say, "The arc of the universe is long, but it bends towards justice." The key thing is to focus on Jesus. The devil works by distracting us from what really matters.

✳ ✳ ✳

We wrestle not against flesh and blood. (Ephesians 6:12, KJV)

A rod is easier to bend when it is still wet.
(Setswana, Botswana)

＊

Most people would agree that adults in general are "smarter" than children. But try to teach both an adult and a child a foreign language, and you will discover that the child picks it up much more quickly. The same is true of a musical instrument or physical activity such as dancing. The child has fewer preformed notions or bad habits—in other words, less "baggage" to get in the way.

This same dynamic applies to the area of discipline. In fact, many traditional African cultures maintain that the education of a child begins in the womb. That is why the spiritual, physical, and psychological state of the mother and of the expecting family are critical to the health of the child.

Habits are formed early. Therefore, be active and progressive in shaping a child's mental and physical universe. Rearing children begins and ends with this: the reverence and praise of God. Do not refrain from asking elders what to avoid and what to plan for. Elders and children have an intimate relationship. The place where the children are going is the place that the elders have just come from.

＊   ＊   ＊

[Hannah] made this vow: "O LORD of hosts, if only you will look on the misery of your servant, and remember me, and not forget your servant, but will give to your servant a male child, then I will set him before you as a nazirite until the day of his death. He shall drink neither wine nor intoxicants, and no razor shall touch his head." (I Samuel 1:11, NRSV)

An okra tree does not grow taller than its master.
(Ghana)

＊

My recent rereading of Mark Twain's *Pudd'nhead Wilson* caused me to reflect on the main character, Tom, who in his adulthood had failed to shed the rotten, uncouth, selfish ways of his youth. I could not help but wonder how many young people like Tom are in our churches, schools, workplaces, and neighborhoods today. There is nothing more unattractive and repulsive than a person exercising hubris, expressing reckless disregard toward elders, and becoming prideful toward those who are responsible for his or her education.

Brilliant youth, beware. Smart students, take heed. Intellectual prodigies, watch out. Do not try to outdo those whom God has positioned to serve you in capacities of authority. Do not outdo yourself in trying to show off your gifts. This is a poor waste of time, energy, brilliance, and creativity.

Do not regard yourself as superior to those whose duty it is to see to your well-being, health, and education. Respect the process of growth. If an okra tree outdoes its master, who will be there to shape, nourish, and protect it from hazardous storms? Furthermore, other masters will probably shy away. We all need teachers and elders; that is why, in the Bible, no one is referred to as an adult. We are all children of our Father in heaven. It resonates well with this proverb from Ghana. The brother or sister who does not respect the traditions of the elders will not be allowed to eat with the elders.

＊　＊　＊

"The disciple is not above his master, nor the servant above his lord. It is enough for the disciple that he be as his master, and the servant as his lord. If they have called the master of the house Beelzebub, how much more shall they call them of his household?" (Matthew 10:24-25, KJV)

Only the feet of the voyager know the path.
(East Africa)

✳

Experience is the reward for honest effort. It does not come lightly; it comes to those whose lives have been forged in the crucible of challenge. That is why it has become almost a truism that "experience is the best teacher."

Consult those who have been there. Do not try to reinvent the wheel or recreate the table. For information, rely on people who have given their life to certain things. Knowledge is attained and sustained through doing. Ability is attained by ways of action. There is almost no other way.

Revelation is hardly an instantaneous process. Most revelations come through hard work, effort, consistency, and challenge. What appears to be immediate and sudden is often the result of long-suffering. Try not to be like a shooting star that brightens the sky for a moment and is seen no more. Be instead like the sun: slow to rise, but once risen, remaining in place for its appointed time.

*　*　*

Listen, children, to a father's instruction,
    and be attentive, that you may gain insight;
for I give you good precepts:
    do not forsake my teaching.
When I was a son with my father,
    tender, and my mother's favorite,
he taught me, and said to me,
    "Let your heart hold fast my words;
keep my commandments, and live." (Proverbs 4:1-4, NRSV)

63

Don't look where you fell but where you slipped.
(Nigeria)

＊

Failure is the stuff of a faithful life. However, it is not its finish—victory is. Perhaps that's why Deborah McGriff, a Detroit teacher, once said to her students, "Treat failure as practice shots." There is indeed a season for everything under the sun. As night follows day, victory is sure to follow defeat. Growth always involves the risk of desire being thwarted. There is a time to weep, but after the season of mourning comes the time to revise, correct, and regroup.

Many can solve the problems of others, but few have mastered the art of self-examination. We focus on the symptoms of our failings (because such exercises inescapably lead to integrity and humility) and not the cause. In one of Jesus's parables, the caretaker who asked for more time was forced to dig up (as well as expose and expurgate) the roots of the fruitless fig tree (Luke 13:6-9). If we focus only on the symptoms and do not deal with underlying causes, we will commit the same mistakes over and over again.

Many people enter into serial relationships, not because there is something wrong with others, but because something is wrong with them. Healing is not found in changing partners.

＊　　＊　　＊

"When an evil spirit comes out of a man, it goes through arid places seeking rest and does not find it. Then it says, 'I will return to the house I left.' When it arrives it finds the house swept clean and put in order. Then it goes and takes seven other spirits more wicked than itself, and they go in and live there. And the final condition of that man is worse than the first." (Luke 11:24-26, NIV)

One flees from the roaring lion to the crouching lion.
(Sechuana)

✳

Fear is False Evidence Appearing Real. It is common knowledge in East Africa that the lion that roars the loudest is the least mobile lion. It roars more out of anxiety and depression than out of courage and strength. The crouching lion, however, is strong and agile. The point is for the lion who gives the roar to drive the prey in the direction of the crouching lion.

This is also the tool of the adversary of faith. Fear paralyzes us and draws us near danger. It traps us. That is why wise hunters say, "Run toward the roar." Face the challenge, because fear confronted leads to great faith.

* * *

There is a tide in the affairs of men
Which taken at the flood, leads on to fortune;
Omitted, all the voyage of their life
Is bound in shallows
And miseries.
On such a full sea we are now afloat,
And we must take the current when it serves,
Or lose our ventures.

—William Shakespeare

* * *

I remind you to rekindle the gift of God that is within you through the laying on of my hands; for God did not give us a spirit of cowardice, but rather a spirit of power and of love and of self-discipline. Do not be ashamed, then, of the testimony about our Lord or of me his prisoner, but join with me in suffering for the gospel, relying on the power of God… (2 Timothy 1:6-8, NRSV)

It takes a whole village to raise a child.
(West Africa)

✳

Some sayings are popular. This one is profound. Most people would agree that children owe a lot to their parents. However, the most able parents that I have spoken to often admit that solid childraising is simply overwhelming on their own. More often than not, successful parenting is rooted in strong ties to a wider moral community or family of faith.

Jesus grew up in the home of Joseph and Mary. However, he was raised in the synagogues and the temple courts. The village concept of child development highlights group faith, collective commitment, and corporate sacrifice.

The paralytic's friends showed remarkable care, concern, and commitment in bringing the sick man to Jesus. Luke writes that their faith—the man's and his friends'—moved Jesus to forgive and heal (Luke 5:20). This is the same ethical principle that should apply to childraising. Children do not belong to us but to God, who gives them to the world as blessings. The community bears the burdens that the parents alone cannot.

Our African ancestors were wise enough to know that the nuclear family is an insufficient mechanism for raising a child, especially during these times when we are being pulled and pushed by the pressures of modern existence. Biology is not the only key to a well-disciplined and developed adult; sociology and spirituality are just as important. The greatest village for the nurturing of our children is the church, the house of prayer, the city of God, the body of Christ.

* * *

After three days they found him [Jesus] in the temple, sitting among the teachers, listening to them and asking them questions. And all who heard him were amazed at his understanding and his answers. (Luke 2:46-47, NRSV)

He who hides his disease cannot be cured.
(Ethiopia)

✳

Disease is dis-ease. Paralysis. It comes with our fallen condition. We cannot go through life without being infected. It happens to all of us—the best and the rest, the wise and the unwise. Yet some people are able to emerge triumphant from its weakening vagaries, while others seem plagued for life.

While there are some diseases that are degenerative, many are curable. Neither psychological nor physical diseases are beyond God's power to heal, yet most healings take place only if the sick person has identified and exposed his hurt, wounds, sickness, and disease. If no one knows your hurt, you cannot be helped. The blind man cried out for mercy. The woman with the issue of blood left her home and found Jesus at the center of the town. Jesus healed the man with the withered hand under the scrutiny of the unfriendly Pharisees.

* * *

Confess your sins to each other and pray for each other so that you may be healed. The prayer of a righteous man is powerful and effective. (James 5:16, NIV)

The young cannot teach tradition to the old.
(Nigeria)

✳

Life, creativity, energy, passion—young people promise much but lack experience. The obligation of the young is to learn. The knowledge they can gain from the old is hard-won bounty that the young dismiss to their hurt. Unfortunately, the strength of the young, which is a fresh vision for the future, works against their receptivity to the tried paths of previous generations.

The obligation of the old is to teach. The obligation of the young is to learn. To confuse these two roles is to invite disaster to any people or nation. The old know how and why certain truth has been revealed in particular times and places, where God brought them through. They expect that God will bring them through by sure ways again. At the outset, those who have gone before have a duty to impart the benefits of their experience to newcomers. It is their duty to God.

* * *

These commandments that I give you today are to be upon your hearts. Impress them on your children. Talk about them when you sit at home and when you walk along the road, when you lie down and when you get up. Tie them as symbols on your hands and bind them on your foreheads. Write them on the doorframes of your houses and on your gates. (Deuteronomy 6:6-9, NIV)

While you erect a fence, also dig a pit.

✳

A capable thief always spots several exits from his place of operation. A social predator finds multiple ways to attack her prey. Why make their jobs easier?

In traditional African communities, fences are necessary, yet they are hardly sufficient. Pits serve as a backup. When the fence fails or falls, you can take refuge in the pit.

We take refuge in God. The proverb holds true for physical life, but in the spiritual realm—at the foot of the cross—God is the first and the last.

*　　*　　*

I waited patiently for the LORD;
  he inclined to me and heard
     my cry.
He drew me up from the
     desolate pit,
  out of the miry bog,
and set my feet upon a rock,
    making my steps secure.
He put a new song in my mouth,
    a song of praise to our God.
Many will see and fear,
    and put their trust in the LORD.
(Psalm 40:1-3, NRSV)

You can bend a tree or orient its course only when it is very young.
(Cameroon)

✳

According to the law of heliotropism, plants grow toward the light. So it is with a young tree. A young tree is always flexible enough that one can bend it or orient its direction of growth in life. But when the tree is mature, it becomes stiff. It sometimes resists and defies even the storm. It becomes hard to bend. Forget about attempting to map out its course.

The same holds true for childrearing. When a child is still a babe, that is the time when parents and the community should influence the child's future. The moral or ethical values inculcated and nurtured in a child live on in adulthood. The child grows up with them. If we wait until a child who is dangerous to society hits twelve before our reform machinery is sought or summoned, it is too late. Such an effort would be bound up in "shallows and miseries." As we make the beds of our children, so must they lie on them.

* * *

Train children in the right way,
    and when old, they will not stray. (Proverbs 22:6, NRSV)

Away from home, learning is one's mother.
(Yoruba)

✳

Mother-learning has taught me:
- You cannot make someone love you; all you can do is work on your love for God.
- Forgiveness is easier said than done. Yet it is worth doing.
- No matter how much I care, some people just do not care back.
- One of the surest paths to misery is to try to please everybody.
- It is not what you have in your life but the kind of life you have that counts.
- Ignorance is a short path to the deep pit of damnation.
- It is insane to throw dirt into your own eyes in order to make someone else look good.
- When working for the Kingdom of God, blisters turn into bliss.

*   *   *

My child, keep my words and store up my commandments with you; keep my commandments and live, keep my teachings as the apple of your eye; bind them on your fingers, write them on the tablet of your heart. Say to wisdom, "You are my sister," and call insight your intimate friend. (Proverbs 7:1-4, NRSV)

**Until grief is restored in the West as the starting place where
the man and woman might find peace, the culture will
continue to abuse and ignore the power of water,
and in turn will be fascinated with fire.**
(Burkino Faso, Malidoma Patrice Somé, *The Healing Wisdom of Africa*)

✳

Westerners, on the whole, cannot claim to have suffered as have those who
live in undeveloped nations. This wise saying suggests a willful ignorance on
the part of westerners of the value of feeling profoundly what it means to be
human, which is to know grief. People with leisure and affluence have the
ability to avoid having to feel vulnerable. Westerners seem to think of themselves as potent influencers and conquerors. Those are dynamisms that
might be likened to fire.

Water is a connecting element. To start with grief in finding peace means
to seek a life of connection and integration. In the womb, a child is conceived
as a nascent being, which grows in a watery sac into a fully limbed infant-
child, ready for birthing through anguish and water. Water presents that
basic challenge of integrating pain with living.

Fascination with fire is instinctively a draw to that which consumes,
which leaves no trace of living, breathing, hurting flesh. Fire does not so
much speak of grace as it does of determination and sudden fury.

Grief beckons human beings to belong to each other, but not for the purpose of taking advantage of vulnerabilities. The call is toward service in the
name of peace, with the knowledge that every heart has its story of pain.

* * *

Finally, all of you, have unity of spirit, sympathy, love for one another, a tender
heart, and a humble mind. (I Peter 3:8, NRSV)

The day never turns back again.
(West Africa)

✳

I imagine saying something like this:

> Dear Father Time,
>
> Oh, how we abuse your precious privilege. We have been given so much of you, but alas, we beat our breasts and complain that there are never enough hours in the day.
>
> Signed, "The Human Race"

Does not God present us with time? Are we not to use this awesome blessing according to God's glory and purpose? How we invest our time is an index of our stewardship, a marker of our spiritual maturity. How one spends time today will be told tomorrow. That is why we must "think now against the day," according to a Nigerian proverb.

Imagine how many blessings we have missed because we have failed to invest in the bank of time. Time is a precious gift, a resource that cannot be recycled. The use of time speaks more to our character than almost anything else. Jesus' public ministry lasted less than three years. Consider the work of his hands during that time.

* * *

Teach us to count our days
   that we may gain a wise heart. (Psalm 90:12, NRSV)

* * *

Do not love sleep or you will grow poor. (Proverbs 20:13, NIV)

If you try without being successful, your day of fortune has not yet come.
(Dagomba)

✳

Scripture reveals plainly that the godly reap their reward in due season. "To everything there is a season, and a time to every purpose under the heaven" (Ecclesiastes 3:1, KJV). "Teach us to number our days, that we may apply our hearts unto wisdom" (Psalm 90:12, KJV). "A faithful man shall abound with blessings: but he that maketh haste to be rich shall not be innocent" (Proverbs 28:20, KJV).

The fact that your harvest does not come when you expect it is not proof that it is not on God's schedule. The "in between" time is your "in the meantime." The waiting time is the working time. It is not the time to fear but the time to have patience. Patience is the capacity to work where you are expecting something.

The old farmers in my father's hometown of Abeokuta, Nigeria, always found something constructive to do during a drought. They knew that the harvest would eventually come, and so they took its unpredictability as a divine charter to engage in other forms of labor in anticipation of the hour of deliverance.

* * *

Let us hold fast the profession of our faith without wavering; (for he is faithful that promised). (Hebrews 10:23, KJV)

* * *

[Jesus] said to them, "Why are you sleeping? Get up and pray that you may not come into the time of trial." (Luke 22:46, NRSV)

Critique does not depreciate the sweetness of honey.
(West Africa)

✳

Walking is universal. So is criticism. But walking is action, and criticism is reaction. Reactions, by nature, rarely change the initial act.

It has been said that a cynic is one who knows the price of everything and the value of nothing. A cynic, therefore, is one who is more obsessed with his or her own opinions than with reality.

The Efik of Nigeria say, "Every rose has a thorn as its friend." The poor criticize. The rich criticize. Children criticize. Adults criticize. Since criticism is a universal affair, it is best to focus solely on what God has sent you to Earth to do. No amount of criticism can derail the blessing and brilliance of God's work through your hands. No enemies can destroy the dimension of providence that is designed especially for you.

* * *

It is a fearful thing to fall into the hands of the living God. But recall those earlier days when, after you had been enlightened, you endured a hard struggle with sufferings, sometimes being publicly exposed to abuse and persecution, and sometimes being partners with those so treated. For you had compassion for those who were in prison, and you cheerfully accepted the plundering of your possessions, knowing that you yourselves possessed something better and more lasting. Do not, therefore, abandon that confidence of yours; it brings a great reward. For you need endurance, so that when you have done the will of God, you may receive what was promised. For yet "in a very little while, the one who is coming will come and will not delay; but my righteous one will live by faith. My soul takes no pleasure in anyone who shrinks back." (Hebrews 10:31-38, NRSV)

Looking at the king's mouth, you will never think he sucked his mother's breast.
(Nigeria)

✳

Heights can be deceiving. Their appearance changes with the perspective of the viewer. The heights of prestige and privilege are no different. Those who occupy social heights are often viewed inaccurately by adoring crowds.

To regard another human being with too much awe and adoration is to practice idolatry. Inevitably this means that we are prevented from worshiping God in spirit and in truth. On the other hand, not to recognize how far people have come is foolhardy. What is required in interpreting all human affairs is balance of perception.

In many traditional African societies, the king is regarded as the symbol of God's power on Earth. In the past, the ruler often exercised absolute authority over a given geographic region. However, according to the elders, even the king is human and has fallen short of the glory of God. Even the king had to suck, to learn, to grow. David was not always the salutary authority who marshaled his troops to victory after victory on foreign battlefields. Solomon had to be trained to become the most powerful ruler on Earth. Even God entered the human situation as a child born into a manger.

Let us respect authority without losing sight of the frailty, fallibility, and finitude of those who manage the conditions under which we live and labor. The path to leadership is long and arduous. It is also a divine calling.

* * *

Jesus increased in wisdom and in years, and in divine and human favor. (Luke 2:52, NRSV)

People do not wash their eyes before getting into a fight.

✳

We may not enter into a fight with someone if we have taken time to look into the matter with which we take issue. Having a clearer vision, or "clean eyes," could well mean there would not be a fight at all.

Foretelling is risky business. Who among us knows when or how trials will come? It is good policy not to blame those who have fallen into trouble. God is often working within the mess to bring forth a miracle. Spiritual people are able to discern this work where others see fatality. The key is to intercede on their behalf. The tongue cannot blame and bless at the same time. All have sinned and have come short of God's glory.

Our ancestors said that God sits up high but looks down low. He is all we need to get by. The human drama is the stage of holy deliverance. Tragedy is often a stepping-stone to triumph. Crisis in God's hands inevitability gives birth to creativity. Do not be overly judgmental of people who face hard times. Every person who has lived a life worth living has had to endure a storm.

* * *

Don't be afraid. Am I in the place of God? You intended to harm me, but God intended it for good to accomplish what is now being done, the saving of many lives. (Genesis 50:19-20, NIV)

* * *

The stone the builders rejected
   has become the capstone. (Luke 20:17, NIV)

He who runs after good fortune runs away from peace.

✳

They call him Savior for a reason. He satisfies. He gets the job done. But he will not violate the canons of our freedom in order to get to us. We must assent. We must participate. The apostle Paul put it this way: "It is by grace you have been saved, *through faith*" (Ephesians 2:8, NIV, italics mine). Grace is God's part; faith is our part. Faith is not the absence of fear but the ability to face fear.

The pursuit of money is our culture's way of handling fear. "Money will solve our problems," fear declares. "If we could just get a better job," doubt says. "If only I could get that dream condo," anxiety announces. Too many of us worship the god of hedonism, bowing at the altar of desire.

The biblical wisdom is still true: "The love of money is the root of all evil" (1 Timothy 6:10, KJV). Though many in today's world, including some Christians, try to find a way around this text, there is no denying the fact that money is a fleeting entity. To love money is to pursue it above all other human needs. We must not put profit over people, nor the material over the moral. Christ came to save people, not money.

* * *

The house of the righteous contains great treasure,
　　but the income of the wicked brings them trouble.
　　(Proverbs 15:6, NIV)

If you wait for somebody, you will eat in the night.
(West Africa)

❋

From birth, most Christians are taught that selfishness is a bad thing, a vice to be overcome. In contemporary parlance, we speak of a culture of narcissism and a need to curb our runaway individualism. More than a few social commentators have bewailed the age of entitlement. No doubt there is sufficient Christian teaching on the virtues of conforming to group rules, working within set guidelines, sacrificing for others. But are there times when the ideals of sacrifice and conformity become vices? Should single-mindedness be lifted up? Is self-care to be denounced? Does unwarranted sacrifice lead to suicide? Where would the church be without the focused faith of the monks? How about the rugged, audacious, impassioned individuality of the apostle Paul?

In many traditional African cultures, there is an ever-present dose of realism that accompanies moral teaching. Each person is called to a specific task that is custom-made to fit that person's personality and temperament. This task becomes one's source of living. As Billie Holiday once said, "Papa may have, and mama may have, but God bless the child that got his own."

*   *   *

Be careful ... how you live, not as unwise people but as wise, making the most of the time, because the days are evil. (Ephesians 5:15-16, NRSV)

One who sees wealth for the first time buys a mad cow.
(Igbo)

✳

Strange paradox: those who make the most often owe the most. One writer has said that we live in an over-spent society. Our spirits become drained in the race to acquire. We moderns have mastered how to get money but not how to use money. We make it and then it makes us. Certainly money does not make us crazy, but it can provide the opportunity to express irrational behavior.

When one becomes suddenly rich, one spends money on useless things. This means that one's wealth is quickly transferred to another. In fact, one way that the wise rich recognize the not-so-wise rich is through the use of money. Many lottery winners have gone broke soon after their big payday because they have failed to learn how to grow their money. Plan for the future in things that bring positive rewards. Before you get good money, get the good mentality.

* * *

Poverty and disgrace are for the one who ignores instruction,
but one who heeds reproof is honored. (Proverbs 13:18, NRSV)

When I did not have cattle, I did not sleep.
Now that I own cattle, I cannot sleep.
(Setswana)

✳

Fear governs the appetites. One day, we live *to* get. The next day, we live *for* what we have gotten. The thing that makes you live is often the thing that makes you die. What you work so hard to own may one day own you.

Does money bring happiness? Maybe. Folks that I know who are rich and happy share one cardinal conviction: Their contentment does not come from the ownership of money. It comes from devoting their lives to a greater pursuit whose by-product is pecuniary benefit.

Remember the fourfold virtues of Job: he was a man of integrity; he was just; he feared God and refrained from evil. Though he was wealthy, the Bible does not connect his virtuous character to the possession of things. This suggests that his faithfulness in the midst of adversity had much to do with his relationship with God.

Let's take a lesson from the life of this great man of Uz. The acquisition of money bequeaths new problems that were hidden during the time of poverty. Perhaps that is why Solomon prayed for wisdom rather than wealth (2 Chronicles 1:8-12). The ownership of wealth without wisdom soon makes a poor soul. Let us not only *believe in* God; let us simply *believe* God.

* * *

We look not at the things which are seen, but at the things which are not seen; for the things which are seen are temporal, but the things which are not seen are eternal. (2 Corinthians 4:18, NASB)

* * *

Perfect love casteth out fear. (1 John 4:18, KJV)

It is the calm and silent water that drowns a man.
(Nigeria)

✳

Gwendolyn Brooks says, "We lurk late, we thin gin." Easiness dulls the senses, weakens the wit. Be on the lookout. What appears to be harmless and innocuous may be a mask for something greater, something deeper, something larger. Check out these images: the serpent, the apple, Adam and Eve, Samson and Delilah, Noah's drunkenness, David and Bathsheba, Isaac and Jacob. How often are we trapped by the appearance of godliness? How often are we suckered into another bite of the proverbial apple? We must constantly and vigorously be on the lookout for what lies beneath.

*   *   *

Do not be wise in your own eyes;
　　fear the LORD, and turn away from evil.
It will be a healing for your flesh
　　and a refreshment for your body. (Proverbs 3:7-8, NRSV)

*   *   *

With persuasive words she led him astray;
　　she seduced him with her smooth talk.
All at once he followed her
　　like an ox going to the slaughter,
like a deer stepping into a noose
　　till an arrow pierces his liver,
like a bird darting into a snare,
　　little knowing it will cost him his life. (Proverbs 7:21-23, NIV)

Children of the same mother do not always agree.
(Yoruba)

✳

Look at the record: Cain and Abel. Jacob and Esau. Joseph and his brothers. Jephthah and his half-brothers.

Let me make five observations:

1. If it is true that siblings do not always agree, then we shouldn't expect to agree with strangers.
2. Biblical siblings who disagreed had major imperfections, yet God used them.
3. We may not all agree, but we can still love each other.
4. Do not expect people to be perfect.
5. The perfect church is still in the making.

Look to Jesus.

* * *

A friend loves at all times. (Proverbs 17:17, NRSV)

If a furuncle swells up inside your mouth, you will have to swallow some of the pus.
(Cameroon)

✳

No matter where a boil swells up on the body, it is painful. Relief comes only when the boil has been emptied. When the furuncle is inside the mouth, one has no choice but to swallow the pus that comes through the saliva.

And so it is with life. Sometimes we involuntarily find ourselves in situations beyond our control, wherein we are forced to face certain challenges that we would otherwise never tolerate. This demands fortitude and bravery on our part, resources to breast the challenge. Eric Copage has said, "In every adversity, look for the benefit that can come out of it. Even bad experiences offer benefits, but you have to look for them."

* * *

Five times I received from the Jews thirty-nine lashes. Three times I was beaten with rods, once I was stoned, three times I was shipwrecked, a night and a day I have spent in the deep. I have been on frequent journeys, in dangers from rivers, dangers from robbers, dangers from my countrymen, dangers from the Gentiles, dangers in the city, dangers in the wilderness, dangers on the sea, dangers among false brethren; I have been in labor and hardship, through many sleepless nights, in hunger and thirst, often without food, in cold and exposure. Apart from such external things, there is the daily pressure on me of concern for all the churches. Who is weak without my being weak? Who is led into sin without my intense concern?

If I have to boast, I will boast of what pertains to my weakness. (2 Corinthians II:24-30, NASB)

In God's shrine, this world,
what everybody wants is a good life.
Why do people always make trouble?
God has given principles to live by,
but only you yourself can follow them.
(Dogon)

＊

The esteemed theologian, Paul Tillich, reputedly was asked whether he believed in absolute truth. He replied, "Yes, if it owns you. No, if you own it." So much religious intolerance, so many denominational fights, so many church splits occur because someone believes that they alone have cornered the market on God's will and services. Few pause to think that such a prideful attitude flies in the face of God's overwhelming love. A story by Klyne Snodgrass illustrates the point:

"Once the Devil was walking along with one of his cohorts. They saw a man ahead of them pick up something shiny. 'What did he find?' asked the cohort. 'A piece of the truth,' the Devil replied. 'Doesn't it bother you that he found a piece of the truth?' asked the cohort. 'No,' said the Devil, 'I will see to it that he makes a religion out of it.'"[1]

＊　＊　＊

You must understand this, my beloved: let everyone be quick to listen, slow to speak, slow to anger. (James 1:9, NRSV)

---

1. Klyne Snodgrass, *Between Two Truths—Living with Biblical Tensions* (Zondervan: 1990), 35.

Long ago did not live long ago.
(Zimbabwe)

✳

The preacher says, "What has been is what will be, and what has been done is what will be done; there is nothing new under the sun" (Ecclesiastes 1:9, NRSV). Some very fundamental things under the sun have been and always will be present, because human needs—arising from the agony and glory of living—are constant at the core of our being and existence in the world. We repeatedly must do those things that tend toward sustaining life and meeting human needs for shelter, nourishment, growth, creativity, and discovery.

Long ago does well to stick around, because the life actions that require wisdom from every age are familiar here and now. The generation coming up in these days lacks an historical memory. World events unfold at a dizzying pace, with the constant and excessive access we have to news reporting, and days are too crammed with stimulus to sort out one from the next. We postmoderns experience daily what might have been once-in-a-lifetime events in a different age. I am certain that I have lived many lifetimes, if change is the measurement, by comparison with someone living even 100 years ago.

Even so, today is the era of long ago for those who know the value of wisdom. And of course, wisdom owes its agelessness to timelessness. Long ago lives in the present, because wisdom for living is daily available to us under the same sun that has lighted the world since the beginning of time.

* * *

Those who love me, I will deliver; I will protect those who know my name. When they call to me, I will answer them; I will be with them in trouble, I will rescue them and honor them. With long life I will satisfy them, and show them my salvation. (Psalm 91:14-16, NRSV)

If you go about searching for something and you find yourself where you've been before, certainly you'll not find what you're searching for.

✳

When you can't find your wallet, should you wallow tirelessly in your back pocket? Is it possible to eat meat with a straw? Do you go to pigs to learn cleanliness? We often live life in the wrong lane, drive on a highway going in the wrong direction, and use inaccurate maps. Too often we get stuck in conflict zones, become codependent, and become paralyzed by doubt when we refuse to look beyond our immediate circumstances. Life on planet Earth is characterized by stress and storm. Yet to fret over difficulties beyond our control compounds life's problems. The key is to develop the courage to change the things you can and "press on toward the goal for the prize of the heavenly call of God in Christ Jesus" (Philippians 3:13, NRSV).

* * *

"Go ... to the lost sheep of the house of Israel. And as ye go, preach, saying, The kingdom of heaven is at hand. Heal the sick, cleanse the lepers, raise the dead, cast out devils: freely ye have received, freely give. Provide neither gold, nor silver, nor brass in your purses. Nor scrip for your journey, neither two coats, neither shoes, nor yet staves: for the workman is worthy of his meat. And into whatsoever city or town ye shall enter, enquire who in it is worthy; and there abide till ye go thence. And when ye come into an house, salute it. And if the house be worthy, let your peace come upon it: but if it be not worthy, let your peace return to you. And whosoever shall not receive you, nor hear your words, when ye depart out of that house or city, shake off the dust of your feet. Verily I say unto you, It shall be more tolerable for the land of Sodom and Gomorrha in the day of judgment, than for that city." (Matthew 10:6-15, KJV)

The welcome gestures of a dog with a short or no tail is hardly known or appreciated by the master.
(Nigeria)

✳

Love is a verb. It must be acted out, expressed, manifested. The desire of every person is to experience something. Perhaps all of us find it hard to appreciate the affection of a dog with a short tail.

The most visible action of a dog's unspoken words of welcome to the master is the swift and enthusiastic wagging of the tail. The story is different with a dog who does not have a tail or who has a short tail. It is not always enough that the dog runs toward the master when the latter is arriving home.

This is the story of the poor, the weak, and the lowly in society. Irrespective of the quality of their love, admiration, support, and respect for the nobles, the privileged, the rich, and the highly placed in society, the latter never know or appreciate them. Someone has beautifully said that the generosity of the poor is hidden in the heart. The widow's mite of the poor or weak means little or nothing to the beneficiary.

We should learn to appreciate everybody just as he or she is. We should acknowledge the otherness of others. After all, if everybody were a king or queen, who would be the subjects? We are *all* created in the image of God.

* * *

Did not God choose those who are poor in the world to be rich in faith and heirs of the kingdom that he promised to those who love him? (James 2:5, NAB)

* * *

We urge you, brothers, admonish the idle, cheer the fainthearted, support the weak, be patient with all. (I Thessalonians 5:14, NAB)

When people are successful in life, the foolish claim the credit.

✳

Does a successful investor create the interest she collects? Does a farmer cause his crop to grow? Both work hard, but they also depend on things beyond their control. Wise people realize that they are always helped by circumstance and by God, but fools nurse a different story about their success in life. They claim the credit. They maintain that they did it and got it. They throw God out of the picture. They become preoccupied with their own success.

This proverb defends the sovereignty of God. It affirms the role of God in every human affair. It validates God as the author of providence. It speaks for God—a God who is all-powerful; a God who is neither known nor comprehended by fools, even by fools who have been made successful in life by the God whom they know not. Wrapped inside every success is the silent voice of God—sometimes unheard or ignored—saying: "It is my making." Without God's approval, we cannot do anything. There is no success without God's signature.

* * *

Fools say in their hearts, "There is no God." They are corrupt, they do abominable deeds; there is no one who does good. (Psalm 14:1, NRSV)

PART SEVEN

"His Eye Is on the Sparrow":

The Divine-Human Relationship

God does not leave God's child tied up overnight.

❋

"He's an on-time God. Yes, he is." So thundered the lead singer's voice through the AM banner on the radio.

Expecting a word from God? Remember, God may not come when you want, but God is always right on time. God never fails. God never loses a case. God has never lost a patient. The Psalms reminds us that God never slumbers nor sleeps (Psalm 121:3-4).

If you are a believer, have faith in this: Nights inevitably turn into morning, a valley is just a landing dock for a victory between two high points called mountains, and every sickness is not unto death. The key point is to pray for endurance and for enlightenment. As one preacher said, "When your hands are tied—that's praying position."

*   *   *

About midnight Paul and Silas were praying and singing hymns to God, and the prisoners were listening to them. (Acts 16:25, NRSV)

When your enemy digs a grave for you, God provides an emergency exit.

✳

Haman set up Mordecai. He was to die on the gallows. But Haman's scheme backfired. He was caught, and the Scriptures say that "they hanged Haman on the gallows he had prepared for Mordecai" (Esther 7:10, NIV). Resist the devil and he will flee, but if you flirt with him, he will rule.

Some rules of thumb: First, try not to work against any of God's people. Second, if you are on the receiving end of punishment, trust in God. Third, remember that in a grave your enemy can't hear you and you cannot hear anyone. This sharpens the spiritual antenna and makes one trust in the One who can transform the tomb into a womb. And remember that God also provides a rescue team, and God likes to perform in style. Expect something miraculous through an unseen door.

*   *   *

God is my shield, who saves the upright in heart. (Psalm 7:10, NRSV)

The world measures but God sews.

✳

It has been said that when we make plans, God laughs. I think that God laughs at us—period. "We propose, but God disposes" was a saying I constantly heard during my youth in Nigeria. Human beings make plans, but only God has the capacity to deliver. Recall the words of the psalmist:

Unless the LORD builds the house,
    its builders labor in vain.
Unless the LORD watches over the city,
    the watchmen stand guard in vain. (Psalm 127:1, NIV)

Always include God in even the smallest of plans. Do not exclude God from any area of your life. Bring God in on the decision to choose the wallpaper, if you have to. God sees and knows everything. God is a wonderful and forgiving parent. Among the things that the Father likes best is to hear from his children.

* * *

Trust in the LORD with all your heart,
    and do not rely on your own insight.
In all your ways acknowledge him,
    and he will make straight your paths. (Proverbs 3:5-6, NRSV)

One does not forego sleeping because of the possibility of nightmares.

✳

You want to dream. But to dream you must sleep. Not to explore possibilities because of the risk of nightmares is to turn life itself into a nightmare. Every venture worth engaging in involves untold and incalculable risks. Faith takes risks.

Remember a particularly compelling nightmare, a brutal affair. Remember one who from birth was marked for death. He had to flee from his place of birth. His enemies launched a smear campaign about him. His own people never readily understood him, if at all. His friends contradicted him. He was arrested on a trumped-up charge, slapped, beaten, scourged, humiliated, betrayed, denied, murdered. Yet, he bore it all for you and for me. Was it worth it?

Thank God that by living through a nightmare and by turning it into resurrection, God in Christ took away our own nightmares. You and I have been given work to do. Problems are what we see only when our eyes are taken away from the work and purpose. We see obstacles when we take our eyes off of the prize. Nothing prodigious is accomplished by constant aversion of one's eyes, out of fear.

* * *

There is no fear in love, but perfect love casts out fear; for fear has to do with punishment, and whoever fears has not reached perfection in love. (I John 4:18, NRSV)

Do good and your reward will be with God.
(Hausa)

✳

Instant gratification has become the mantra of our global culture. Sacrifice, on the other hand, is a rare commodity. It was also rare in the days of Jesus.

One day James and John allowed their egos to get the best of them. Scheming for privilege and status, they said to the Master, "Grant us to sit, one at your right hand and one at your left" (Mark 10:37, NRSV). Sounds kind of arrogant. But let's not condemn the disciples from our modern vantage point. We moderns live in a global rat race. We, too, want to be recognized, rewarded, and promoted. We may do well to hear Jesus' reply to James and John: "Whoever wishes to become great among you must be your servant" (verse 43).

We must learn to serve, to let *goodness* be our mantra. God in heaven sees us and rewards our faithfulness. Many good deeds are met with thankless hearts in this world, but the reward of a Christian's work is found in God. This is the only reason why we should perform our Christian duty. We do not strive for the praise of human beings but to do a work wholly acceptable and pleasing to God.

Jesus understood the hearts of individuals. He did not appeal to their goodwill, nor did he seek their praise. His food was to do the will of his Father. It was his Father who rewarded him. God will reward those who trust God by giving them life—and life more abundantly. Faith is not a fetish; it is the fruit of spiritual warfare.

* * *

If you abide in me, and my words abide in you, ask for whatever you wish, and it will be done for you. My Father is glorified by this, that you bear much fruit and become my disciples. (John 15:7-8, NRSV)

The owner of a cheerful heart will find joy ever increasing.
(Swahili)

✳

Recently, I went on a worldwide tour. I discovered one thing: I never left the world of my own soul. There was one thing common to all of my experiences—Me, Myself, and I! I discovered that what I experienced was greatly influenced by my own feelings. This led me to conclude that a joyful countenance has little to do with one's age, occupation, ethnic background, or political party. One's joy is a matter of feeling comfortable with God's choices, with the hidden plan of God.

My birth, who my parents are, my ethnic background, the people who come into my life are all things God has freely ordained, making no mistakes. Joy is finding out what is pleasing to God from knowing God's Word. His Word sets me free and purifies me. I can choose to set my life toward God's choices or I can choose not to be so aligned. I can choose life or death.

Wherever I go, into my own backyard or all the way to the waters of the Nile or to the slopes of Mt. Everest, I cannot leave myself. The essence of my travels boils down to this: joy is self-discovery through God-discovery.

* * *

Rejoice in the Lord always; again I will say, Rejoice. Let your gentleness be known to everyone. The Lord is near. Do not worry about anything, but in everything by prayer and supplication with thanksgiving let your requests be made known to God. And the peace of God, which surpasses all understanding, will guard your hearts and your minds in Christ Jesus. Finally, beloved, whatever is true, whatever is honorable, whatever is just, whatever is pure, whatever is pleasing, whatever is commendable, if there is any excellence and if there is anything worthy of praise, think about these things. (Philippians 4:4-8, NRSV)

Where they think of God, God is not there.

✳

"Resurrection," in the words of the late, great Dr. Miles Jones, "is life where life ain't supposed to be." It is possible to live again. After all, God is a God of new beginnings. To be a Christian is to experience resurrection. That is why Jesus told Nicodemus, "You must be born again" (John 3:7, NKJV). In other words, resurrection is the capacity to die to something and to begin a new walk in Christ Jesus.

Joseph died a certain death. So did Moses. And many preachers have given testimony to the resurrection. People who are not expected to survive will always do so by the power of God.

We must recognize that God's ways are not our ways. We cannot put God in a box, because the moment we do that, our expectations are certain to be exploded. The renowned theologian J. B. Phillips wrote a book entitled *Your God Is Too Small.* South Africans found a new interethnic orientation. Nelson Mandela found freedom after four decades in jail. Martin Luther King renewed and deepened his commitment to human liberation after a brutal knife wound to the heart. Remember, the women went to the tomb to find Jesus, but he was not there.

*   *   *

The women were terrified and bowed their faces to the ground, but the men said to them, "Why do you look for the living among the dead? He is not here, but has risen. Remember how he told you, while he was still in Galilee." (Luke 24:5-6, NRSV)

*   *   *

The LORD is good to those who wait for him,
   to the soul that seeks him. (Lamentations 3:25, NRSV)

No one has to teach a child that God exists. (Twi)

❋

Parent and child go together. The relationship exists by definition. We exist in relationship—physically, socially, and spiritually. Just as it is absurd to teach a child that the breast from which it sucks does not exist, so it is absurd for a child to deny the existence of God. You cannot deny the existence of the one who created and sustains you. This holds true with reference to one's human and spiritual parenthood.

Among many peoples in Africa, it is believed that God-consciousness is not taught. It is preset in the subconscious of the child. It is ingrained in the psyche of the fetus. In short, simply by being alive, we know that God is. The infinite mercies of God are paraded in the beauties of creation. The grand signature of God permeates the fauna and flora of the Earth. God is present to the senses and the spirit. That is why many Africans are astounded by the claim that before the coming of foreigners Africans had no God.

*   *   *

When Elizabeth heard Mary's greeting, the child leaped in her womb. And Elizabeth was filled with the Holy Spirit. (Luke 1:41, NRSV)

If God gives you wealth,
you can even sell ordinary water near the river.
(Waja)

✳

Criticism. Accept it. You're going to get it. One need not fear the criticism or envy of human beings. No one can take away the blessing God has for you. Your destiny carries with it the divine imprimatur. The Holy Spirit has placed each and every one of us on Earth for a distinct purpose. It is up to us to launch out into deep waters. That is why the Bible says that the just shall live by faith (Habakkuk 2:4). Take refuge in the fact that God rewards goodness and justice and that the righteous are eternally rewarded.

Do not feel guilty for your gifts. Do not be ashamed of your potential. Do not fail to develop the talents God has given you. Too many Christians are ashamed to launch out. God has given us not the spirit of fear but of love and of power and of a sound mind (2 Timothy 1:7).

*   *   *

Go, eat your bread with enjoyment, and drink your wine with a merry heart; for God has long ago approved what you do. (Ecclesiastes 9:7, NRSV)

God will help you if you get up.
(Efik)

✳

I'm constantly amazed at the number of people in the New Testament who were agents of their own empowerment, liberation, or healing. The man at the pool of Bethesda had to pick up his bed and walk. Zacchaeus had to climb a tree in order to see Jesus. The woman with the issue of blood crawled and clawed in order to get to Jesus. Nicodemus had to visit him in secret. The leper had to worship him. The disciples had to follow him. The crowds came to hear him.

This suggests that God requires our participation in the act of kingdom building. God grants us the freedom to choose God or to deny God. For those who choose life, God gives power to be called children of God. Human agency is critical for doing God's work God's way.

* * *

Jesus said to him, "If you are able!—All things can be done for the one who believes." (Mark 9:23, NRSV)

* * *

"Your faith has made you well. Go in peace." (Mark 5:34, NKJV)

God is a great eye.
(Balanda)

❋

No one needs to be in a degree program to learn the fine art of denial. Its messengers are everywhere because it is a consequence of shame. After sinning, Adam used leaves to cover up his body, but he couldn't hide from God. Adam's denial didn't deliver him from sin. The path from denial to deliverance is found only through openness and truth. God sees everything in the world. There is nothing that escapes the divine gaze.

God works through people whom God places in our lives to be instruments of peace. We need to open up to others and experience God's work through them. They are there for support, correction, and reproof. When men and women take the risk and let down barriers, people respond to one another as whole persons and try to communicate with openness and intimacy. This is the stuff from which friendships are formulated and sustained.

God always provides God's children with a mercy seat, with a passport, with an escape route. Often these blessings take the form of other people. With faith and openness, we can proceed with the knowledge that the Father has empowered and enabled us to transform our situation.

* * *

The LORD is thy keeper: the LORD is thy shade upon thy right hand. The sun shall not smite thee by day, nor the moon by night. The LORD shall preserve thee from all evil: he shall preserve thy soul. The LORD shall preserve thy going out and thy coming in from this time forth, and even for evermore. (Psalm 121:5-8, KJV)

* * *

The lamp of the LORD searches the spirit of a man;
it searches out his inmost being. (Proverbs 20:27, NIV)

When a person passes on in a community where a known sorcerer lives, the latter is always the principal accused.
(Cameroon)

Reputations are interesting animals. Bad ones seem to live forever. Good ones seem to live till yesterday. It is an almost universal belief that sorcerers employ devilish, mystical powers to destroy human life. Unexplainable deaths are almost always blamed on them, even when they are wholly innocent.

That is why it is germane to build a healthy reputation for oneself. Someone with a poor record or a notorious reputation in the community is vulnerable to false accusations. What a heavy price to pay when one is not right with God!

* * *

Happy those who do not follow the counsel of the wicked,
Nor go the way of sinners,
   nor sit in company with scoffers.
Rather, the law of the LORD is their joy;
   God's law they study day and night.
They are like a tree planted near streams of water,
   that yields its fruit in season;
Its leaves never wither;
   whatever they do prospers.
But not the wicked!
   They are like chaff driven by the wind.
Therefore the wicked will not survive judgment,
   nor will sinners in the assembly of the just.
The LORD watches over the way of the just,
   but the way of the wicked leads to ruin. (Psalm I, NAB)

A blind man may be told that there is no oil in the soup, but he will have to use his tongue if he wants to find out the level of the salt.

✳

Peter—eager fisherman, rambunctious leader, ambitious servant, passionate preacher—was a *rock*. He started off resisting Jesus' instructions on a boat on the Galilean sea and ended up passionately preaching the gospel of Christ.

Peter came into his own when he fully trusted Jesus. Jesus said, in essence, to Peter and the others, "I have given you basic training. It is time for you to go out and do the work I have trained you for. But remember that your education continues. I will send you another counselor. And he will continue to teach you and help you grow." It was after Jesus had weaned Peter that Peter discovered how to "find the level of salt" on his own. Jesus said to Peter when he washed his feet, "Where I am going, you cannot follow me now; but you will follow afterward." Jesus was growing the disciples' capacity for trust. After Jesus overcame death, he commanded Peter to "feed my sheep," thus commissioning him to shepherd God's people. Peter had tasted the salt and discerned what is pleasing to God. We are charged to do this as well.

We also resist Jesus' instructions. We love being comfortable, unshaken, undisturbed. But God loves us too much to leave us without discipline and duty. To find life, we must give it up, under the guidance of the Holy Spirit. With this strength, we can walk into spiritual darkness, face our fears, and confront the ugly truth about our human condition, and in so doing, transcend it.

* * *

The LORD is my strength and my song, and he has become my salvation; this is my God, and I will praise him, my father's God, and I will exalt him. (Exodus 15:2, RSV)

Index of African Proverbs

21. If your hair is not as long as your friend's, do not plait it like hers. (Nupe)
22. A deer with a long neck tends to get hit by a stray bullet. (Setswana)
23. You cannot hide the smoke of the hut you set on fire. (Burundi)
24. People start preparing for the night when the day is still very young. (Igala)
25. Whose mother is at the pot will not lack soup. (Bwatiye)
26. Lice do not grow on a bald head. (Yoruba)
27. Do not call the forest that shelters you a jungle. (West Africa)
28. One who eats corruption will die corrupted. (Yoruba)
29. The child looks everywhere but does not know what to look for. The old man looks for one thing and sees everything. (Senegal)
30. Lack of knowledge made the hen to sleep on a bundle of corn. (Angas People)
31. To his hosts, the incoming stranger first appeared like gold, then turned to silver, and eventually ended up as crude iron. (Ethiopia)
32. Seeing or spotting an animal in the bush or hunting ground is not tantamount to shooting and killing it. (Cameroon)

PART THREE
"Tell It Like It Is": Human Nature

33. His opinions are like water in the bottom of a canoe, going from side to side.
34. No matter how long a log stays in water, it does not become a crocodile. (West Africa)
35. We work on the surface. The depths are a mystery. (Bahaya)
36. Whoever goes after two termite hills returns empty-handed. (Bahaya)
37. A bird is in the air, but its mind is on the ground. (Mandinka)
38. When the cock is drunk, he forgets about the hawk. (Ashanti)
39. The heart of man and the bottom of the sea are unfathomable. (West Africa)
40. Hunter in pursuit of an elephant does not stop to throw stones at birds. (Uganda)
41. It is an egg that becomes a cock. (Yoruba)
42. Tiger does not have to proclaim its Tigritude. (Wole Soyinka, Nigeria)
43. When two brothers fight, strangers always reap the harvest. (Igbo)

PART FOUR
"Walk Together, Children":
Collective Responsibility and Cooperative Ethics

44. Streams make up a river. (Buji)

45. If you have a stick, no one will bite you.

46. The world has become food for thought. (Igala)

47. The ruin of a nation begins in the homes of its people. (West Africa)

48. One hand cannot lift a thatched roof. (Hausa)

49. When a king has good counselors, his reign is peaceful.

50. It is easier to transport an anthill than to exercise authority in the village. (West Africa)

51. Big fruits fall under big trees. (Tangale)

52. Do not leave a host's house throwing mud in his well. (Zulu)

53. Make no distinction in your behavior between those of rank and the common people. (Ptah Hotep, 2340 B.C.)

54. I am because we are. (East Africa)

55. It is because of the fact that a river flies alone that it meanders. (Tagale)

56. The shoulders are taller than the head.

57. It is often said, "We are"; do not say, "I am."

58. Having a good discussion is like having riches. (Kenya)

PART FIVE
"Mold Me and Make Me": Education and Enlightenment

59. Lice do not grow higher than the head. (Used to describe rebellious children in Igal, West Africa)

60. A rod is easier to bend when it is still wet. (Setswana, Botswana)

61. An okra tree does not grow taller than its master. (Ghana)

62. Only the feet of the voyager know the path. (East Africa)

63. Don't look where you fell but where you slipped. (Nigeria)

64. One flees from the roaring lion to the crouching lion. (Sechuana)

65. It takes a whole village to raise a child. (West Africa)

66. He who hides his disease cannot be cured. (Ethiopia)

67. The young cannot teach tradition to the old. (Nigeria)

68. While you erect a fence, also dig a pit.

69. You can bend a tree or orient its course only when it is very young. (Cameroon)

70. Away from home, learning is one's mother. (Yoruba)

71. Until grief is restored in the West as the starting place where the man and woman might find peace, the culture will continue to abuse and ignore the power of water, and in turn will be fascinated with fire. (Burkino Faso, Malidoma Patrice Somé, *The Healing Wisdom of Africa*)

PART SIX
"Been in the Storm So Long": The Human Dilemma

72. The day never turns back again. (West Africa)

73. If you try without being successful, your day of fortune has not yet come. (Dagomba)

74. Critique does not depreciate the sweetness of honey. (West Africa)

75. Looking at the king's mouth, you will never think he sucked his mother's breast. (Nigeria)

76. People do not wash their eyes before getting into a fight.

77. He who runs after good fortune runs away from peace.

78. If you wait for somebody, you will eat in the night. (West Africa)

79. One who sees wealth for the first time buys a mad cow. (Igbo)

80. When I did not have cattle, I did not sleep. Now that I own cattle, I cannot sleep. (Setswana)

81. It is the calm and silent water that drowns a man. (Nigeria)

82. Children of the same mother do not always agree. (Yoruba)

83. If a furuncle swells up inside your mouth, you will have to swallow some of the pus. (Cameroon)

84. In God's shrine, this world, what everybody wants is a good life. Why do people always make trouble? God has given principles to live by, but only you yourself can follow them. (Dogon)

85. Long ago did not live long ago. (Zimbabwe)

86. If you go about searching for something and you find yourself where you've been before, certainly you'll not find what you're searching for.

87. The welcome gestures of a dog with a short or no tail is hardly known or appreciated by the master. (Nigeria)

88. When people are successful in life, the foolish claim the credit.

PART SEVEN

"His Eye Is on the Sparrow": The Divine-Human Relationship

89. God does not leave God's child tied up overnight.

90. When your enemy digs a grave for you, God provides an emergency exit.

91. The world measures but God sews.

92. One does not forego sleeping because of the possibility of nightmares.

93. Do good and your reward will be with God. (Hausa)

94. The owner of a cheerful heart will find joy ever increasing. (Swahili)

95. Where they think of God, God is not there.

96. No one has to teach a child that God exists. (Twi)

97. If God gives you wealth, you can even sell ordinary water near the river. (Waja)

98. God will help you if you get up. (Efik)

99. God is a great eye. (Balanda)

100. When a person passes on in a community where a known sorcerer lives, the latter is always the principal accused. (Cameroon)

101. A blind man may be told that there is no oil in the soup, but he will have to use his tongue if he wants to find out the level of the salt.

DATE DUE